To Anna-Faith

Stay!

Lit

Lit

Living Christ's Character from the Inside Out

DAVID EDWARDS

Our purpose at Howard Publishing is to:

- *Increase faith* in the hearts of growing Christians
- *Inspire holiness* in the lives of believers
- *Instill hope* in the hearts of struggling people everywhere

Because He's coming again!

Published by Howard Publishing Co., Inc.
3117 North 7th Street, West Monroe, Louisiana 71291-2227

02 03 04 05 06 07 08 09 10 11 10 9 8 7 6 5 4 3 2

Edited by Michele Buckingham
Interior design by Stephanie Denney
Cover design by LinDee Loveland

Library of Congress Cataloging-in-Publication Data

Edwards, David, date
Lit : living Christ's character from the inside out / David Edwards.
p. cm.
Includes bibliographical references.
ISBN: 1-58229-222-1
1. Christian life. I. Title.

BV4501.3 .E394 2002
248.4—dc21

2001051824

Special treatment of words in quoted Scripture was added by the author for emphasis.

To Dortha Ann "Flingie" Edwards,
my first lady of life.
You gave me life,
and your life is a constant example
of how the *lit* life is lived.
I love you, Mom.

CONTENTS

FOREWORD

By Beth Moore

We want it, and we want it fast. Forget snail mail. We can now correspond in seconds and wonder only minutes later why we haven't received a response. Forget a roast baking in the oven. We want to drive up to a metal menu on a pole, yell our order into a faceless speaker, and have dinner delivered when we drive up to the window—our way. If the orders of the two cars in front of us take too long, we'll show them. We'll just pull right over the curb and drive off in a huff and a squeal. No one's going to make us wait!

Except God. The One of whom the psalmist said, "*My times are in Your hand*" (Psalm 31:15). The same One who makes time, takes time.

We occupy Planet Earth during a peculiar dispensation. Modern society is doing its darnedest to take the "wait" out of life. We live in a drive-through society and have simultaneously developed a ravenous appetite for instantaneous gratification. We are so permeated and affected by results-on-demand that if we're going to ascribe to a different mentality, it will have to be entirely on purpose.

God's people assigned to this planet for this moment in time are not unlike their predecessors. If we are to have any level of authenticity in our world, we must be filled with God-given character. Often the reason others aren't buying what we have to say is that they are unconvinced, based on our huge inconsistencies, that we have bought it ourselves. How thankful I am that God stays after us and picks on our inconsistencies until He brings forth a little steadfast character.

I can't think of the issue of godly character without reflecting on 1 Peter 1:7. This powerful verse talks about trials that are allowed in our lives so that God can bring forth something *"more precious than gold which is perishable, even though tested by fire."* What is God's refining goal? That our faith proves genuine. Take a good look at those words. God is driving for something very specific in our lives: He wants to burn the fake out of us. He desires to refine us until no matter where life slices us, we'll bleed Jesus. His job is to stay after us until the character of Christ invades our marrow.

Godly character is achieved only one way: It is built. Thankfully, our Savior is pretty adept with a hammer and nail. He is also patient. Oh, the reality of His patience has been resurrection to my naturally self-destructive life so many times! I have no words to express my gratitude to God for having such patience with me. Perhaps that's how I know He doesn't give up on one of His own. If He did, He would have left me behind a very long time ago. I am a long way from finished, but to the glory of God, I am far from where I started.

I wanted so much to be instantly "fixed." I wanted drive-through healing, drive-through integrity, and drive-through revelation. And don't make me have to put the car in park to get it! I squirmed continually in the discomfort of God's relentless use of time. In the wait, God was gloriously hard at work. I'm still being "fixed," but I'm no longer a fake. How I thank Him for His stubborn love!

Acts 17:26–27 says, *"And He made from one man every nation of mankind to live on all the face of the earth, having determined their appointed times and the boundaries of their habitation, that they would seek God, if perhaps they might grope for Him and find Him, though He is not far from each one of us."* The thought of Dave Edwards inhabiting any other generation makes me laugh out loud. He would have been so shocking to my grandmother's childhood church in Pisgah, Arkansas, that the annual grave cleanin' would have become a significantly larger task. Nope. Dave wasn't meant for any other generation but ours.

I don't doubt, however, that the reverberations of the impact God is having through him will be felt in many generations to come. He is one of a kind. I don't care how many people try to flatter him with imitation, there is only one Dave Edwards. And God has given him something to say. He has called him to feed sheep in our time, and I, for one, like the way he does it.

Admit it. Lots of people can serve up spiritual food, but you don't always enjoy the meal. When Dave serves a meal, you can "*taste and see that the LORD is good*" (Psalm 34:8).

Some people talk in dry meat and bland potatoes. Others talk in macaroni. Still others, a bunch of baloney. This Texan is about to give the ultimate compliment: Dave talks in Tex-Mex. Tasty to the palate. Filling. Spicy. Not too cheesy. And a lot of chili gravy. Yep, Dave's is happy food, indeed. The beauty of it is that later, after the meal, I still know that I've been fed. And before I know it, I want another helping.

Get out of the drive-through lane. Pull on in and stay a while. Don't put this book down until you've gotten all the way to the last page. You won't be sorry. It's a feast.

ACKNOWLEDGMENTS

Writing a book involves more than just one person. In writing this book, I have received invaluable assistance. I would like to thank the following people:

Howard Publishing—John Howard and Philis and Denny Boultinghouse helped in ways that have proven to be more valuable than I could have imagined. When I wrote my first book for Howard Publishing, *One Step Closer,* it contained a chapter on the subject of character. You guys saw the potential for this book before I ever knew I could write it. You challenged me in such a way that a passion for character was stirred within me, the end product of which we now hold in our hands. Thanks, Howard Publishing, for past, present, and future opportunities.

232—Thank you for requiring and inspiring me to write. I remember well when the book "clicked" in my soul: that morning at breakfast when you said, "Every story needs a villain." You taught me that character is all about light and dark. I have called you to talk about this book too many times to count. You welcomed me into your home in the early morning hours to read, discuss, correct, and guide me...and even share with me the benefit of your personal research. Your love and concern for me made this book a reality. Your ministry lives on.

Trey Bowden—No one can turn out a manuscript like you. If it weren't for you, bro, I'd still be sitting at my desk, staring at my yellow pad, and thinking to myself, *Does the apostrophe go in front of or behind the* s?

Bobby McGraw—Thank you for typing all night long, for taking my talks and transcribing them in a way that made them usable for this project. You are the "detail" man.

Andy Savage—Thanks for dreaming and planning and encouraging me to teach these principles after their first "thought genes" were birthed during those long, hot days in Houston. I know how much these truths mean to you personally.

Jay Bruce—My friend across the way, thank you for your help with the project. I miss you much and hope to see you soon.

Memphis Metro (my extended family)—Thank you for letting me "field test" these talks on you and for receiving them with open and willing hearts. Several of the illustrations contained in this book come from the stories of your lives you have shared with me during the "field test." The title for this book came to me as I watched the life of God strike fire in your lives. One more thing—thanks for the new haircut, Karate and Spin.

Prayer Support—Nathan Dalton, you used some of your daily prayer time to pray for me. God heard your prayers for clarity, focus, and endurance. Thanks, man. Carolyn Spurgeon, you quietly lifted me up in prayer for many years before you told me about it. Now I know why I've had the success God has blessed me with. Thank you so much.

John Jernigan—Thank you for taking all the portraits and photos. You've had a personal investment in my ministry since the beginning. You are a true and faithful friend.

Donut People—For telling me it couldn't be done and encouraging me to quit every time I saw you...this came in just for you.

***Lit* Inspirational Soundtrack—**provided by Train, Lifehouse, and Miles Davis.

John Bullard—You are my lifelong *lit* friend who always knows what to say even when I don't know what I need to hear. Keep talking. I'm listening.

INTRODUCTION

A Cause Worth Living For

The first time I connected with the life of Christ was in the backseat of a car. This event, I would later discover, would be the only memorable thing I would ever do in a car's backseat. I remember riding home from church in the car with my mom. Most of the information from the sermon had already left my mind. What stuck with me, however, was the emotional energy of the service. The *power* behind what I had heard still resonated in my nine-year-old soul.

The preacher had closed with the story of a young man who had resisted God's offer of eternal life. Later that day, while crossing the road, this young man had been hit by a tractor and dragged into eternal separation from God.

Aside from the obvious flaw in the story—the young man couldn't dodge a *tractor?* Pavarotti could outrun most farm machinery—the illustration made an impact on my youthful heart.

Stories like this one became legendary during that period of evangelism. Every sermon I heard seemed to include a tale of someone who was killed on a bike or a bus or was otherwise broadsided by some calamity while still in a state of spiritual rejection. These closing illustrations were designed to instill fear in people and motivate them to make an emotional decision for Christ. The effect was not unlike an insurance salesman trying to coerce a reluctant prospect into signing the contract *today*. From the pulpit it sounded like, "Hurry up and come to Jesus so you won't go to hell!"

As a young boy of nine, I cringed at the thought of burning forever in utter darkness. It was an easy decision to make. *Of course* I didn't want to be a crispy critter.

As I rode home that day, I sensed the urgency of faith for the first time in my life. I had been introduced to Christianity with a cause—staying out of hell—and the cause wanted me.

The very next Sunday I walked the aisle to the altar and signed a card. I had my fire insurance now. I would avoid all that burning in the dark.

The knowledge that I had eternal salvation upheld me through my teenage years. But adolescence brought a new cause: discovering and managing my sexuality. All of my faith seemed to rest on my ability to exercise abstinence.

The sermon plots changed. Now they were about young men and women dealing with sexual temptation—some choosing abstinence and some not. The results were similar to the stories in which people were hit and dragged into eternity by tractors.

I faced my share of temptations. Like many other teenagers, I was a kid living in two worlds. I had my teen world, and I had my church world. For a while I struggled to find a way to balance the two. But ultimately, the things of God that I had saturated my heart with for years won out. I chose to make my life in God World.

I was convinced that "true love waits" and "the pure in heart still see God," so I said yes to purity. I remember the ceremony. As we sang "Lord prepare me to be a sanctuary," the words filled the room. My heart soaked up the emotion. I was overwhelmed with the desire to stay pure for God. I walked the aisle to the altar, signed a card, and placed a promise ring on my finger. The cause had me. And it would not be the last cause to come my way.

College brought me into contact with liberal-minded religious people. Their cause was not to have one—a cause, that is. (But isn't "tolerance" a cause in itself?)

I was a religion major studying in a department that was bent on de-Christianizing Christianity. They wanted to remove anything sacred or supernatural from the Bible and privatize the nature of a believer's worship and witness—all in the name of tolerance. They preached, "Love God by accepting everything and everybody, regardless of who they are or what they believe. Above all else, do not confront anyone for any reason." Not only was this cause unappealing to me, it lacked credibility in light of my own personal experience with God. I chose to simply endure those years of liberal study and allow the tolerance cause to pass me by.

During the years that followed, the Christian cause continued to take on many forms. One movement convinced me that I should strive to be "a man of God." A true, godly man was faithful, consistent, and honorable in all his ways—and to make sure of it, we formed accountability groups to monitor each other's behavior. I was given a morality checklist to use as my daily behavior meter, along with a commitment card to acknowledge and solidify my decision to behave like "a man of God." (I signed it, of course.)

I carried the behavior checklist in my wallet and attempted to work with my accountability group. I answered all the questions on the accountability checkup sheet because, after all, "character is what you do when no one is looking."

There have been other causes that have screamed for my attention. When religion and politics collided, I was challenged to protest by carrying signs, writing letters, and boycotting certain institutions. I gave this cause some cursory attention but never joined the march. Many people I know and love felt forced to choose sides and fight. Some of them don't love me now like they did before choosing sides.

Then there were the moral crusades, with certain life habits singled out as the enemies of God. Somehow the "answer" for these struggles of humanity always got reduced to a list of restrictions presented by well-meaning preachers who tended to scream at hurting people, "If you had any character, you wouldn't act this way!" The impression many people formed about the morality cause was based more on their view of the preachers giving the message than the morality of the issue. Many found the delivery of the message offensive. The speakers may have genuinely loved the people they were targeting and rightly loathed sinful behavior. But what the people heard were voices filled with anger, and the natural response was resentment—not a change of heart.

What exactly is going on? Each of these causes rings with a certain amount of truth. But at their root, they are all about modifying people's behavior—about having them *do* something different without having them *be* something different first.

If not doing anything wrong is our goal, we can avoid much wrong through personal discipline and avoiding compromising situations. But what have we really changed? In the end, human effort only affects the *appearance* of a person. God alone has the ability to affect the *character* of a person. True character starts from within and expands outward.

Through the years Christians have been pummeled by a never-ending succession of religious causes. Like waves of the ocean, they will continue to break over us. But causes don't move by themselves; they have to be picked up and moved. That's why every cause recruits followers. No matter how worthy a cause is, it creates followers, not character.

Genuine character is born out of the character of Christ coming to live inside of us. The conversion of our heart is the turning point. It is described in a line from a famous hymn: "I once was blind but now I see." Christ brings light into our dark souls. Like one candle igniting another, His life lights ours. It awakens us. Our souls respond to the word of the Lord: "*Awake, sleeper, and arise from the dead, and Christ will shine on you*" (Ephesians 5:14).

The living light of Christ lights our lives, and new things begin to appear. Peace, freedom, and hope spring out of souls once characterized by uncertainty, bondage, despair, and death.

God's dream is this: that people living the life of God will bring His presence into this earth and insert His re-creating life into a darkened world. No religious event or righteous cause can accomplish what God intends—only the character of Christ working through each one of us.

That's why I have chosen only one cause for my life: having Christ Himself living in me.

This is not a devotional book or theological volume. The stories I tell and the truths I share within these pages are drawn from the life I have carved out both on and off the road. God has birthed these principles in me through very real pain and experience, and I have shared them in talks all across the nation.

There is something in all of us that resents the way things are in the world. And there are definite options for facing the present state of things:

1. We can avoid reality by focusing on our own little world and becoming armchair critics, picking out the imperfections found in the issues and causes of our day as well as in those people who are at least trying to make a difference. If we do this, we end up sitting on the sidelines, sniping at other folks like blow-hard, spiteful cranks.

2. We can look forward to the end of the world, just sitting calmly by, reading the preponderance of doomsday Christian literature on the market while waiting for our escape from this condemned place. But if we do this, we deny the high value God places on His creation, the people in it, and the vital role He has for us to live out as believers.

3. We can choose character. You and I have been given the ability to define ourselves by character. This is the unique power of human beings: to be able to decide what we want our lives to be and what we want to give them to. The decision to pursue character invades all the details of our lives and, over time, becomes obvious to the people around us.

As Christians we have been designated by God to be the light of the world. *"Let your light shine before men in such a way,"* Jesus said in

Matthew 5:16, "*that they may see your good works, and glorify your Father who is in heaven.*" Without us there is no light, and darkness reigns supreme. But with us, the light can dispel the darkness.

Experts agree that reading in the dark is bad for your eyes. As cool as it was reading under the covers with a flashlight as a kid, it was not the optimal reading experience. Reading is much more enjoyable when you don't have to squint. If you read in bad light long enough, you'll find yourself at the eye doctor's office, staring at a chart and asking, "Can I buy a vowel?"

Darkness is not only bad for the eyes; it's bad for the soul. Light, on the other hand, brings understanding and joy. The benefits and virtue of light are joy and connectedness. Throwing a switch and yelling "surprise" initiates a party. Joy and light are never separated.

In a figurative sense, light represents clarity and understanding. We say, "In light of the situation..." or "It came to light that..." or "Let me shed more light on this subject."

No one ever says, "Thank you for shedding darkness on the subject. It's totally unclear now." Darkness manifests itself in fear, anger, and impatience. It makes us blind to God's plans for us and our world. That's why John writes, "*The Light shines in the darkness, and the darkness did not comprehend it*" (John 1:5).

The more light we allow into our lives, the better our comprehension of the world around us. That's certainly true in the physical sense; the light we take in with our eyes helps us to know exactly what's going on. It's also true in a spiritual sense.

This book is concerned with light and its impact on character. It has nothing to do with religious movements, political parties, or moral causes. As Christians, our battle is not with the government, the school system, or the entertainment or fashion industries. And our battle is not between races, cultures, or denominations. We are involved in a much larger battle: the unseen spiritual battle for light that has already eluded too many believers.

Our postmodern generation, like every generation before it, thinks of itself as unique and different. And in many ways we are. But the truth is, you and I have inherited the same dark world that our ancestors knew. We don't have to make excuses for the shape the world is in; it's our inheritance! Neither do we have to feel overwhelmed and defeated by the challenges we face. God has eternal solutions for bringing light into the darkness of every one of the finite conditions we encounter.

This book is not written to everyone: It is written to my generation—postmoderns. Many in the postmodern era have suffered the loss of a transcendent center: Truth, for them, is defined by experience, rather than experience being defined by truth. This book is written to help us understand God's calling to develop His character in our lives.

Which brings up an interesting topic: the power of choice. God never forces anyone to develop His character. Each of us has the opportunity to surrender our lives to the Lord and allow Him to build His character in us as we develop genuine relationship with Him, or we can turn our backs on relationship with Him and choose the darkness. God doesn't ask us to choose character because it will make us better individuals. Character is inseparably connected with God's ultimate purpose and plan for the world. When we choose to develop His character in our lives, we become allies with God in His will for the cosmos and in His ongoing fight against darkness.

Understand that character, as I define it in this book, is much more than the sum total of our values, morals, and behavior. The mainstream definition of character emphasizes our own efforts to adapt our behavior to match our convictions or religious faith. That's not what I'm talking about.

Character is nothing less than *the life of God living in us* in the midst of our everyday encounters with a dark world. Throughout the book I refer to a life of character as a *lit* life. The *lit* life flows naturally when we ask God to come into our lives and work in us, because *His character* is what He is and what He wants to produce in us.

Through the thirteen chapters in this book, I discuss the ongoing spiritual battle we face every day, the concept of character and how it is developed, and practical ways to live out the character of Christ—the *lit* life—every day.

Each chapter concludes with a practical application that I hope you will do more with than just read. These "Spotlight" exercises are designed to help you transfer the truth of each chapter into your everyday experience. In addition, at the end of the book are study questions to help those of you who would like to use this book in a small discussion group or Bible study setting. I have also included questions for individual reflection. The questions correspond to each chapter's content and should provide a springboard for lively discussion.

One more thing. As you will notice, I enjoy humor. It's what I use to deal with the sometimes-harsh realities of life. If you've met me or have ever heard me speak, you know that I like all kinds of humor: jokes, irony, funny illustrations, even sarcasm. As you read this book, please keep in mind that these bits of humor are just that—humor—and they are not meant to offend. They are presented here just as I use them in my talks, to set up and illustrate a truth and make it easier to swallow. I'm convinced that a lot of us need to lighten up. If we fail to see the humor in life, we will surely go insane.

Now that you have some idea of where we're going, turn off that tiny flashlight and turn on a real lamp. It's time to turn the page and begin to learn how to live the *lit* life. As you do, I guarantee the world will see the light of God living in you—and you will not be the only one who is changed.

ONE

Light Fight

HOW THE WORLD GOT THIS WAY

I was having dinner with some friends from another church. "We can't wait until Sunday!" they gushed. They were all pumped up about how great the Sunday services were—great music, great worship, great preaching. But throughout the meal I noticed that any time we started to talk about something spiritual, my friends went back to talking about Sunday. Any topic that had to do with God or faith turned into a conversation about how much they loved the songs, the worship band, and the speaker—on Sunday.

Since I'm always eavesdropping on my own conversations to find a topic for a book or a talk, I thought, *This is interesting*.

A Disconnected Generation

What about days other than Sunday? Is Sunday the only spiritual day? For a great majority of Christians in our generation, there is a *disconnect* between faith and the rest of the week. It has become the norm to separate what we do Sunday at church from what we do the rest of our week. The biggest battle that we are fighting is the separation of faith from life.

As a result, our lives are overwhelmed with a sense of meaninglessness.

Chapter One

We get up, go to work, come home, get up, go to work.... We've got to make money to pay our rent and eat, but there's not much else to it. There's a sense of darkness at the core of the struggling at work, the fighting at home, and the dealing with our own private battles. It all seems to be without purpose.

We have successfully compartmentalized our lives into the little boxes in our date books and disconnected the spirit and life. Faith doesn't fit into the Monday-through-Friday workweek or the Saturday-night-dating boxes. The spiritual dimension is surrounded by the four sides of the Sunday box. As long as it's inside those clearly marked calendar boxes, it makes sense...it thrives and grows. But for many professed believers, the rest of the week is totally disconnected from the first day of the week.

This separation also shows up in terms of character. We tend to think of "character" in terms of self-improvement or changes in behavior—something we control on the surface of our lives.

Tragically, the incentive for character and its relevance to the rest of our lives is lost. It makes sense in church and Bible study, but it doesn't seem to be necessary for the rest of our lives. Christians see people without character getting ahead in life and business. They're dating all the beautiful people, amassing wealth, and taking double-rung leaps on the success ladder. It's tempting for a Christian to believe, "Hey, if they can get by without character, so can I." Our lives fit into a picture that is vastly more important than personal gratification and financial success. But our lives are still the ground where the battle between light and darkness is played out.

Think of the battle between light and darkness as individual special effects that are shot against a green screen, with the final background being dropped in during the editing process. The actors play their parts convincingly, but without the final edited background in place, the theater audience would be left without the full picture.

Recently I saw a documentary about filmmaking. It was amazing to see how the actor performed alone in front of a green screen, anticipating the final background that would be dropped in later. The director hung tennis balls in various places around the sound stage to indicate where certain people and other aspects of the background would eventually show up. Then he and the actor blocked the scene together.

"This tennis ball is your partner, so make sure you recognize him with your eyes," the director said. "*This* tennis ball"—he walked up to another suspended ball—"is a large man with a knife. Avoid him." The director continued until all the tennis balls had been identified. Then the actor went through a couple of practice runs, and the director shouted, "Action!"

Most Christians live their lives like that actor interacting with the pretend people on the sound stage. They read their Bibles, memorize scripture, drink cups of soup for their soul, and never realize that the battle between light and darkness is a very real part of life. To them, the battle is pretend, make-believe, something they don't really have to face. It's something that is dropped in for effect. It'll come together in postproduction.

But there are no tennis balls hanging in the air around us. There is no sound stage, no postproduction. We may only see the green screen; but the battle is real, and so is the enemy. We need to learn to recognize the battle and understand its significance in our day-to-day living.

The Context for the Mess

Our world is in a mess. You don't need me to tell you that. But allow me a paragraph to remind you. Unless you've been in a coma all your life, you know about the killing of the unborn, the increase in crime, the miserable way we're losing the drug war, the violence in the media, the meltdown of the nuclear family, the school shootings, the rise in teenage pregnancy, and a hundred other problems we've pretty much become numb to.

What's going on—and what can we do about it? Is there any kind of protection we can put around our lives to screen out at least some of the mess? Is there some way we can implement a cyber-patrol to keep us from surfing in the wrong places? We're constantly being asked to support the right causes. We do what we can, but our efforts never seem to make much of an impact.

We could offer up lots of reasons for the way things are, but the bottom line is this: There are two competing powers in this world. The Bible tells us that the character of light and the character of darkness have been in conflict since the beginning of time. Everything that happens in our lives and in our world happens in the context of this battle. "*The* Light *shines in the* darkness, *and the darkness did not comprehend* [or overpower] *it*" (John 1:5).

The pain, destruction, and confusion we see every night on the evening news are not the war. They are the symptoms, the signs, of the war. The real battle is taking place *behind* the symptoms, between the character of darkness and the character of light. At times we get overwhelmed thinking about a war of such cosmic proportions. But the truth is, the battle is being played out in some very down-to-earth and often subtle and humorous ways.

Form vs. Function

One sign of the battle is the way we've allowed form to trump function in modern life. We tell kids not to play in traffic, but we sell them ice cream from a moving truck. We say, "Don't kick your little brother," then buy them video games in which the heroes rip the spinal cords out of their opponents. We outlaw toy guns in airports, but we sell real ones at any store ending in "mart."

If you drive a Hummer through the jungle on a mission to retrieve POWs from the enemy's camp, you're playing a part in a heroic action. If you drive a Hummer through the suburbs to retrieve yogurt from the store, you may think you look heroic—but you're just being played.

We spend billions of dollars in medical research to find cures for baldness and male impotence, but we still don't have a cure for cancer, or even the common cold. How backward is that? Somebody's in the dark.

Style vs. Substance

Anytime style—which is *looking* without really *being*—takes over, substance suffers. Why go to the trouble to really *be* something if just *looking* like something is good enough? WWF "wrestling" is the perfect example of style over substance. It is pretending to hit without really hitting. It's also pretending to entertain without being entertaining. That's what I call "substance abuse."

Style believes that it is better to look good than to actually be good. Politicians spend so much time, energy, and money telling us how authentic they are and how much they really care about us that they don't have any time, energy, or money left to demonstrate either one.

Look at the music world. It's all about promotion. Many bands are created by businessmen with deep pockets and a vested interest in the success of a particular record label. The groups are carefully marketed to create a need in the public for their particular "product." Such bands aren't formed by sincere, self-taught musicians in a garage down the street. They don't rise to greatness because of their own artistic abilities. They are glorified karaoke singers singing songs written by professional songwriters, choreographed by professional dancers, and marketed by professional advertising executives. Their success is about as fake as the material their clothes are made of. They're good-looking because they're meant to be seen more than heard. Millions of dollars are spent on developing their images and enhancing their bodies through the miracle of cosmetic surgery. These "entertainers" have more plastic on them than a Corvette.

Greed vs. Goodness

In a world where most forms of sin carry health hazards, greed seems to be the last "safe" indulgence. Greed is a game that is played to see how much "stuff" can be accumulated, and more of us are playing than ever before. There have never been more millionaires in the world than there are today. For many of us, the quest for money is the driving motivation for existence.

If you're caught up in the game of greed and think you're doing pretty well, let me put it in perspective for you: Bill Gates is worth ninety billion dollars. He wins! The rest of the nation comes in a distant second.

Greed is also alive and well in the city of God. Flip through the channels and listen to the preaching shows, and it always comes back around to money. The preachers look sincerely into the camera and say, "This is a nondenominational ministry." But I've seen their eyes light up at the sight of tens and twenties!

Stupification vs. Smarts

Education in America is being increasingly "dumbed down." The following are some sample math questions demonstrating this dumbing-down factor:

From a 1960s math test: "A logger cuts and sells a truckload of lumber for $100. His cost of production is 4/5 of that amount. What is his profit?"

From a 1980s math test: "A logger cuts and sells a truckload of lumber for $100. His cost is $80, and his profit is $20. Find and circle the number 20."

From a math test in 2002: "An unenlightened logger cuts down a beautiful stand of trees in order to make a $20 profit. Write an essay about how that makes you feel. Include a paragraph about how it makes the birds and squirrels feel."

The basic skills necessary to function successfully in our world were once taught in our schools. But today more effort seems to be put into affirming a student's self-worth than teaching reading, writing, and arithmetic.

Knowing is not always better than not knowing. Sometimes knowing causes more heartache because we don't know what to do. In the remainder of this chapter, I want to define the problem we face and set up the rest of the book so that you can know the vital role character plays when dealing with this mess we call our world.

The Cosmic Mafia

There are many names for the enemy. For our purposes in this book, think of Satan and his fallen angels as the cosmic Mafia. Although there is no specific Scripture describing the exact prehistoric events of the rebellion of Lucifer, most of the church fathers, beginning with Jerome, agree that Scripture does present the fall of Satan and his demonic army.

Here's how it all began. Before the Garden of Eden was created, when the globe was void and without light, there was a rebellion in heaven. Satan was called Lucifer back then, and he was one of the top three angels (along with Gabriel and Michael). He decided he wanted God's job.

"God," Lucifer boasted, "I'm going to take Your job, and I'm going to be like You. I'm going to sit on Your throne." The end result was that God said, "Let me think about that…NO!" He expelled Lucifer and a third of the angels from heaven. Many scholars believe that the fourteenth chapter of the Book of Isaiah transcends its description of an earthly king. From the earliest times of the church, this passage has been understood as presenting Satan and his angels falling like lightning from the sky to the earth, where he set up his cosmic Mafia and staked out the earth as his territory.

> *How you have fallen from heaven, O star of the morning, son of the dawn! You have been cut down to the earth, you who have weakened the nations! But you said in your heart, "I will ascend to heaven; I will raise my throne above the stars of God…. I will ascend above the heights of the clouds; I will make myself like the Most High."* (Isaiah 14:12–14)

Jesus validated Isaiah's vision of the prehistoric fall of Satan when He reported in Luke 10:18, *"I was watching Satan fall from heaven like lightning."* And a great many scholars agree that Revelation 12:4 refers to this same great fall: *"And his tail swept away a third of the stars of heaven and threw them to the earth."*

We're going to discover how to recognize the enemy and later how to fight him. It's important to avoid extremes when dealing with the enemy. It's important to never underestimate or overestimate the presence of darkness. Three things will help us keep it all in perspective.

1. The Cosmic Mafia Has One Leader and Many Fallen Angels

The devil doesn't have all power. He can't be everywhere at once. Like Tony on *The Sopranos*, he's the godfather commanding the bosses, captains, and foot soldiers. They have staked out territory all around the globe. (I know *The Sopranos* is an HBO show, but it continues to draw more than eleven million viewers each week…so I know at least some of my readers have seen it.)

Even though his power is limited, Satan still has considerable influence that must be recognized and dealt with. The apostle Paul helps us with this understanding in Ephesians 6:11–12, where we are told, "*Put on the full armor of God, so that you will be able to stand firm against the schemes of the devil. For our struggle is not against flesh and blood, but against the* rulers, *against the* powers, *against the world* forces *of this darkness, against the spiritual forces of wickedness*."

Satan's presence on the earth and his influence on the creation and people is observed in Scripture. In Job 1:7 we read, "*The LORD said to Satan, 'From where do you come?' Then Satan answered the LORD and said, 'From roaming about on the earth and walking around on it.'*"

Satan has access to the created world and the people in it. Paul reflects this same thought in Ephesians 2:2: "*You formerly walked according to the course of this world, according to the prince of the power of the air, of the spirit that is now working in the sons of disobedience*." Paul is saying that before Christ enters any life, that life is lived according to the rules of darkness—the darkness that is ruled by the prince of the power of the air, Satan. That life is ruled by the cosmic Mafia.

First John 5:19 tells us that "*the whole world lies in the power of the evil one*." Even though Jesus has come into the world and died for the sins of mankind and "*whosoever believes in Him*," the world still lies in the power of the evil one.

2. The Cosmic Mafia Is the Source of Evil

All the evil that is in our world comes from the syndicate of darkness. The context for the mess in our world is darkness. The person behind the darkness is the enemy. All evil, all tragedy, and all hurt come from the evil one.

Rebellion was created in the heart of Satan. His leadership of the rebellion in heaven is proof enough of this. God did not create this evil; it was created in the heart of this evil one. Ezekiel 28:15–16 demonstrates this clearly when God says to Satan, "*You were blameless in your ways from the day you were created until unrighteousness was found in you.... You were internally filled with violence, and you sinned; therefore I have cast you as profane from the mountain of God.*" This rebellious one was cast out of heaven to the earth, where he introduced evil into the world through the sin of pride in Adam and Eve, and he continues to propagate evil throughout the world.

We have mistakenly believed a lie that some evil comes from God—that God has some ultimate good planned for the evil that comes into our lives. The truth is, God can't be all good and be the instigator of evil. The instant He causes one evil thing, even with a purpose of ultimate goodness, He becomes a part of evil.

3. The Cosmic Mafia Has the Ability to Affect the Future

In Matthew 4, Jesus was led into the desert to be tempted with everything Satan possessed. Satan took Jesus to a high place and taunted Him, "Bow down to me, and I'll give you all the kingdoms." Commenting on this passage, Bible scholar A. T. Robertson says, "The devil claims the rule of the world, not merely of Palestine or of the Roman Empire. 'The Kingdoms of the cosmos' were under his sway.... Jesus does not deny the grip of the devil on the world of men."[1] And Donald A. Hagner, in *Word Biblical Commentary*, explains that when Satan offers "*all the kingdoms of the world and their glory*" (Matthew 4:8), he means "this world and all its wealth" or "all that this world has to offer."[2]

At that instant in time, every kingdom from every different point of the future was compressed into one moment. Satan wasn't pointing to one little parcel of land and offering it to Jesus. What Satan was saying to Jesus was, "I'm showing you the history of mankind before it happens, and everything you see now and forever I will give to you for one moment of your affection."

What's interesting about this story is that Jesus never said, "You can't give me that." Jesus never disputed the fact that Satan and his cosmic Mafia have the power and rule over the kingdoms of the world. The cosmic Mafia controls the world. We live in the mob's world.

I can hear the question, so let me ask it for you: "Yes, but hasn't the enemy been defeated?" We are taught that the enemy has been defeated, and we try to hold on to this as the end-all promise when dealing with the enemy. The only problem is, our everyday experience tells us something very different about our enemy. We face him and his influence, we experience his power, and we try to hold on to that promise but find it's like trying to rappel with dental floss. It might be long enough, but we don't trust it.

The enemy has been defeated, but so have the Dallas Cowboys and the L. A. Clippers. They're not real championship contenders, but other teams still have to play them in their schedules. Wile E. Coyote still sets his ACME traps, and the Road Runner still has to face them. Any team that takes the Cowboys or the Clippers for granted could add a loss to their record. And the Road Runner still has to use everything at his disposal to outwit the coyote.

God placed man in the midst of the Garden to fulfill more than a caretaker role. God created man perfect and sinless so that the earth could be completely filled with God's presence.

Because of the fall of man in Genesis 3, God's master plan now includes the rescue of all humanity, as shown in the following promise made by God in the Garden of Eden: "*And I will put enmity between you and the woman, and between your seed and her seed; he shall bruise you on the head, and you shall bruise him on the heel*" (Genesis 3:15). God's master plan now includes the recreation of mankind. "*For God so loved the world, that He gave His only begotten Son, that whoever believes in Him shall not perish, but have eternal life*" (John 3:16). All mankind has the potential to be salvaged through the proactive actions of Christ on the cross.

It is in this setting that Satan's plan of counterattack can be seen. Our enemy is still very real, with real power. Never forget that to take him for granted is to grant him to take you wherever he chooses.

The Competing Master Plan

> *The Light shines in the darkness, and the darkness did not comprehend* [or overpower] *it.... He was in the world, and the world was made through Him, and the world did not know Him.* (John 1:5, 10)

The mob is conspiring to keep us in darkness, to hurt us, to make us stumble, and to undo whatever God is doing in our lives. This is the competing master plan. God's master plan is to fill the earth with His light through the *lit* lives of His people. Satan's plan is to deconstruct everything God has created.

The cosmic Mafia knows that it can't kill believers because they belong to the Lord. But it can cripple them. So it sets up and launches well-planned attacks. These are the battles we fight.

Many Christians ask, "Why is it that I gain a little ground and then lose a little ground in my spiritual walk? Make some progress, then fall back? Why do I do well for a while, then get pulled off course?" It's because there is a competing master plan. There is a power of darkness battling against the light. For everything God does in our lives that is rich and good, Satan has a counterplan to deconstruct it and take it away.

We have been taught to be fatalists. See if you recognize any of these words from your own thinking:

"Well, if it's meant to be, it will happen."

"If it's God's will, it will come to pass."

"If God is in it, it will work."

That's fatalism. Of course God's will is at work in the world, but there is a force, a cosmic Mafia, an enemy with a competing master plan. The agenda is to undo everything that God does in the lives of individuals in Bible studies, in churches, in relationships, in jobs, careers, and projects. When things don't go the way we expect them to, we have got to resist the urge to think, *Well, God must hate me. He must be out to punish me. That good thing that didn't happen must not have been His will for me.* We've got to see that such thoughts originate in darkness and are meant to keep our minds in darkness.

Deconstruction works best in darkness, as I found out one night not too long ago. It used to be that "pulling an all-nighter" meant that I stayed up and studied through the night. Now that I'm older, it means that I didn't have to get up and go to the bathroom at 3:00 A.M. Anyway, on this particular night I didn't make it to the morning. I pretty much know where everything is in my house, but as I shuffled to the bathroom in the dark, I rammed my toe into the corner of something that didn't budge.

The kind of pain I experienced is time-released. At first it doesn't hurt, but you say to yourself, "This is going to hurt in just a minute." You can almost do the countdown to the pain. "Oh yeah, there it is, right...there." When you're half asleep it can take a minute for the signal to get from your toe to your brain and then get distributed to every nerve in your body. "Owwwwww!"

This is how the darkness works. It slowly layers gray on gray, gradually blinding people until they finally realize they've been crippled in their spiritual progress. It deconstructs their walk with God so imperceptibly that they don't realize they've gotten off the road until they reach the edge of the cliff.

The Countercultural Messiah

> *And the Word became flesh, and dwelt among us, and we saw His glory, glory as of the only begotten from the Father, full of grace and truth.* (John 1:14)

Enter the Messiah. Jesus came to counter the cosmic Mafia and its master plan. Everything Jesus did on this earth was done to drive out the darkness. That's why He healed people, cast out demons, opened blind eyes, and raised the dead. He wasn't showing off in order to win bar bets all over the country. He didn't do these things so He could sign autographs with "Jesus, the Messiah." Nope! He came and did these things to establish and extend the kingdom of God.

The presence of darkness was symbolized by people's blindness, demon possession, physical death, and all manner of sickness. These were the places where darkness lived, and these were the places where Jesus stepped in.

Turn on a light, and it radiates throughout the room. Invite Jesus into any dark situation, and His light penetrates the darkness—whether that darkness has settled into bodies or souls.

Why does this concept consistently escape us? Why do we try to separate the spiritual and the physical? And why do we always treat the symptoms instead of applying the cure?

An over-the-counter cold remedy may temporarily relieve the symptoms of a stuffy nose and allow you to get through a few hours relatively comfortably; but sooner or later the medicine wears off, and you end up blowing through a box of tissues quicker than some repeat offenders go through second and third chances. Treating cold symptoms doesn't cure the cold; it just masks the symptoms until the cold runs its course. In the same way, expending a lot of energy fighting the symptoms of darkness does nothing to drive out darkness; darkness just bides its time and eventually shows up somewhere else.

Wherever Jesus stepped into darkness, there was no place for it to hide. Out of His character and into these situations the light flowed and the darkness fled. Because the enemy had been thrown to earth, Jesus became flesh. God in the form of Jesus Christ came to this world. He died on earth because the battle had to be fought on the enemy's turf.

Both the power of darkness and the power of light chose the cross. Darkness saw the cross as a tool of ultimate defeat for God and His master plan. But the Messiah chose the cross as the weapon that would release the invading light of His person and character into the syndicate of darkness. Let's look at what Jesus did when He dealt Satan his fatal blow.

He Destroyed the Works of the Enemy

> *The Light shines in the darkness, and the darkness did not comprehend* [or overpower] *it.* (John 1:5)

Light always overcomes the darkness. Jesus, who is Light, came into this world and overpowered the darkness, destroying the works of the enemy wherever He went. He didn't just put a Band-Aid over the physical struggles of the people, addressing only the *symptoms* of darkness. He destroyed the very *cause* of darkness, which was the enemy himself. Jesus faced Satan in mortal combat—and won. He was declared the winner by God, and the enemy had to run. Darkness can now be seen for what it is: evil. And as the light of Christ is revealed to us, we have the opportunity to experience a new kind of life.

He Restored Order and Light

> *But as many as received Him, to them He gave the right to become children of God.* (John 1:12)

Jesus took on all the sins, scars, and mess-ups of humanity and made them His own. He received all of the darkness of the world and carried it with Him to the cross. There He hung between earth and sky and died a cruel, slow, suffocating death. Then, with His last breath, He hoisted himself up and declared, "It is finished."

What was finished? Darkness! The Messiah of Light defeated Satan on his own terms and turf. And Satan is still defeated. Now we have the freedom to live in the light of Christ and experience a life that has order and purpose, the way God always intended.

Character Mandate

> *In Him was life, and the life was the Light of men.* (John 1:4)

We are not innocent bystanders in this battle. There is no middle ground. Everything is divided between light and darkness. Each of us must choose sides. "*But as many as received Him, to them He gave the right to become children of God*" (John 1:12).

We have established that the world is in darkness. There is a way for our world to be *lit* with the life of God: It happens when people choose to take on the character of Christ. The only hope for true, worldwide change is when the light of Christ is seen through people who have taken on the character of Christ.

The overriding mandate for us as Christians is to be the light of this world. This is what character is all about. If we are to fulfill this mandate, we must make choices in our lives based on the light of Christ that dwells within us.

God places a great value on humanity and our role in His cosmic master plan. To choose character means that we choose to fulfill God's plan not just *for* our lives but *with* our lives. Through this choice we advance the light of God into the world, dispelling the darkness. To not choose the character of God is to choose to leave the world in its current, darkened state.

As we've said, the devil has been defeated—in principle. Now we must defeat him in practice. We must choose to live a life that is countercultural, that goes against the prevailing rule of darkness in the world. We must choose to live like Jesus did. And when we do, we can expect the same results. Our lives will impact the lives of those around us.

In this book I define "character" as *the life of God living in us*. Every time we make a decision based on the light of God in us, we shine light on the darkness. We see evil for what it is. And when we choose not to let evil control our lives and choose instead to do what is right, we create an environment where darkness cannot survive. Darkness is defeated!

Which brings us back to my friends at the restaurant. (Yes, there really is a connection.) Our lives are created to be *lit* every day. We need to see life for what it really is. We need to be excited about connecting with life the way God intends us to live it. It's an everyday thing.

You may be content to leave all things spiritual in the Sunday calendar box. We all have the freedom to choose between maintaining the status quo or taking up the challenge to live *lit* lives. The mandate is clear, and the choice is yours. Are you ready to get *lit?*

Beginning a Quiet Revolution

Imagine that in the days when Jesus walked through Galilee, a satellite was orbiting the earth. Now imagine that a giant mirror on the satellite was able to reflect the light of Christ into the lives of the people He touched, while a giant camera photographed these individual pin-points of light. The light of each pinpoint would not be significant in itself. But place that pinpoint of light near five others, and it would have some significance. Place those six near twenty-five others, and there would be a growing reduction in the darkness.

Think of it. What if every street, every city, every suburb, every school, every church, and every business were filled with the light of Christ because the believers within them chose to live obedient, *lit* lives filled with the character of Christ? That's God's master plan: for so many people to be filled with the light of Jesus that darkness has no place to hide!

Character is not just about how you do business, what you do when no one is looking, or the rules you use for proper societal behavior. It's more important than that. You are to be the light of your family, your work, your neighborhood, and your company. Character is about each of us *being* the light, destroying darkness, and restoring life as God intended it to be.

But something has gone horribly wrong. And it keeps this vision from becoming a reality.

Purchase a nice candle and place it in your home or office. Light it every day as a reminder of your mandate: to live a life *lit* by the character of Christ in you.

TWO

Wrecked Light

WHY WE ARE THE WAY WE ARE

We are by nature gardeners. Some till the soil and plant the seed. Others fill a caretaker role. My gardening experience is limited to the thirty-seven-item salad bar marked "Garden Fresh."

In the beginning, God placed Adam and Eve in a perfect garden and surrounded them with lush plants and a vast array of animals. Today we call settings like this the zoo. Every animal and plant has a brass identification plate. In many ways, we are just like Adam; we have an innate desire to rule and to bring order to creation. I guess that's why we trim our bushes into animal shapes and give Chia Pets as the perfect gift at Christmas.

God created Adam and Eve in His image and placed them in the garden called Eden. As spiritual beings they had God's nature and were created to never die. They were "all good" beings with awesome power to choose and rule. They were given the task of making the whole earth a garden of God's presence. Their assignment was to literally "Edenize" the entire world.

Our role as gardeners is a sacred, holy, God-ordained role. We are God's gardeners and are charged with the same task as Adam and Eve. We are to bring God's light into every part of our lives. We are to live *lit* lives that drive out the darkness and turn the enemy's ground into Immanuel's ground.

It is impossible to understand the importance of character without first realizing everything that was lost in the Garden. Something went horribly wrong with Adam and Eve, and it continues to impact us all today. What went wrong prevented them and us from living out our God-given design.

The godfather of the cosmic Mafia made Adam and Eve a deal they thought they couldn't walk away from. The moment they took the deal, the light of God was extinguished from their lives. They fell from light into the darkness. They lost their eternity, their authority, and their relationship with God, along with their birthright. They also lost the character of God's light, and they took on the character and identification of darkness.

There is nothing good about this news. In fact there's not enough light in this picture for Thomas Kinkade to do anything with. From all appearances, God's plan to bring His light to the world through mankind was finished.

It is important that we gain a clear perception of what our nature was like before redemption. This is the only way we can have a clear vision of who Christ is within us. In his book *The Spirit of the Disciplines: Understanding How God Changes Lives*, Dallas Willard writes, "Without an understanding of our nature and purpose, we cannot have a proper understanding of redemption. Do we need to know so much about our own nature before we understand how that nature can change through salvation? Yes."[1]

Each of us is fundamentally identified with the same darkness Adam and Eve traded God's light for. Left unchanged, each of us is capable of incredible acts of evil. In Romans 1, the apostle Paul lays out the stages leading up to the demonstration of evil acts. His vivid word pictures show how each stage gets darker than the last.

We've said that *lit* is "the life of God living in us." This is a book about becoming the person of Jesus. And that involves more than wearing a WWJD bracelet. It is more than character in a moral sense.

It is more than self-improvement or being a better person. According to the Bible, character is the life of God coming to live in us. That is something we can't start; we can't stoke that flame. It is something God must ignite. He must take the steps to put His character within us.

As God steps out of heaven and steps into our hearts, we literally take on the presence of God. It's not a game of pretending like we have His character. It is more than acting like we're different. He literally re-creates us. We become someone we were not before. Our darkness is replaced with His light. What literally happens is that we take on the Spirit of God Himself. We become *lit!* We don't create it; *He* creates it in us. *He* steps out of heaven. *He* steps into our hearts. *He* makes us alive from the inside out.

This is all well and good for those of us who have been *lit*. But we still live in a world that specializes in dealing out hurt. Sometimes it seems the person was right when he sang, "Only the good die young."

Evil Examined

The question people ask most when confronted with the effects of evil is, "How could anyone do this?" If you're alive (and who reading this isn't?) you've been faced with genuine evil. It could be that you've taken tremendous hits in your relationships. You fell in love with someone who didn't just hurt you a little; he or she hurt you a lot. You walked away from the relationship thinking, *How could someone do something like that?* Someone who professed to be moral, a church attender, someone who claimed to love God and country—how could this person do something so despicable to another human being? Many of us have walked out of relationships with serious injury to our souls.

I know many who have grown up in households where they watched their parents fight it out. Their homes would experience the extremes from utter chaos to absolute silence. The moment the screaming stopped and the silence began, they knew it didn't mean that things were at peace. It just meant that the house was in a cold war. Their parents were two people who professed their love for each other, yet something was terribly wrong.

Chapter Two

Many of us have lived through the bombing of our homes. Your parents called a family meeting and dropped it on you: "It's over. I'm leaving your mom." Or, "I'm leaving your dad." There you sat, wondering how somebody who was such a good man, such a good woman, could do anything to hurt his or her family.

Back out a little bit from your own life and look at our country and some of the horrible things going on in it. As I write this book, three recent events have topped America's "Why do these things happen?" list. It wasn't that long ago that an African-American boy was dragged to his death behind a truck with a rope tied around his neck. Then there was the senseless, horrific crucifixion of Matthew Shepherd. This young man was put into a vehicle and driven out of town, where he was literally crucified on a fence and left there to die. Then in June of 2001, Andrea Yates, a Houston mother of five, drowned all five of her children. She is claiming a defense plea of insanity, citing extreme postpartum depression, especially after the birth of her last two children. Questions surround this event, and we struggle to understand how a mother could murder her own kids. These are just three examples of evil done in a country that claims to be "one nation under God." Many are asking, "Where is God?"

While this book was in the process of being edited, terrorists attacked the twin towers of the World Trade Center. They hijacked four commercial airliners and with two of them rammed the twin towers. They flew another into the Pentagon building. The fourth hijacked airliner was crashed in a remote area of Pennsylvania. Cleanup will take months and multiplied millions of dollars to complete. The devastation brought to human lives will take much more than money and a great deal longer to repair. Evil is no longer an ambiguous entity in our world; it has a face, and these brief descriptions have provided us with an up close and intimate look.

In his book *Martyrs and Fighters: The Epic of the Warsaw Ghetto*, Philip Friedman relates an eyewitness account of evil done to a young Jewish girl named Zosia living in the Warsaw ghetto during the Nazi occupation. This young girl was the daughter of a physician. During one of the ghetto raids, some of the German soldiers saw Zosia and were captivated by her beautiful, diamond-like dark eyes.

"I could make two rings out of them," said one of the soldiers, "one for myself and one for my wife."

His colleague held the girl.

"Let's see whether they are really so beautiful. And better yet, let's examine them in our hands."

Laughter broke out among the soldiers. The little girl's eyes widened in terror as one of the soldiers twisted out the words, "Let's take out her eyes." A shrill, childish scream pierced the noisy laughter of the soldier pack.[2]

Even now, the screaming penetrates our brains and pierces our hearts, and the laughter cuts like a bayonet plunged into our bodies. We awaken to the reality that we can't possibly understand evil apart from the faces, names, and experiences that incarnate it. Anything short of our facing evil incarnate dilutes our complete understanding of how important a role we play in God's plan to light our world.

I live in Oklahoma City. Oklahoma City is famous for the 1995 bombing of the Murrah Federal Office Building. Everyone saw it on TV; CNN covered it twenty-four hours a day. What the camera lens couldn't show was that even after two weeks, fifteen bodies still had not been found. For two weeks those bodies were in the rubble, and several blocks of downtown smelled like rotting flesh. It was horrific. That one evil act turned downtown Oklahoma City into a war zone. How could a man just drive up in a truck and blow up a building? How could he just get into another car and drive off as if it were no big deal? How could something like that happen? How could somebody do something like that?

Our country has had a rash of shootings on school campuses that are too numerous to name. Fifth graders, sixth graders, seventh graders, eighth graders are pulling the trigger on their classmates. It's very normal for people to ask, "Where is God in all of this?" We go to church and sing our songs; then we look at all the tragedy, all the heartache, and all the turmoil and ask, "If God is such a loving God, why is all of this happening?"

If you flip on the news anytime some tragedy happens, the news anchors all ask the same question: "How could someone do something like this?" There is a plethora of excuses and reasons that they give. They look to culture, to entertainment, to media. The critics stand up and say, "If there really is a God, then why is this happening?"

I saw a news report about a guy who held up a convenience store and afterward shot a customer who was pumping gas. The reporter interviewed a person on the scene who said, "I guess the customer was at the wrong place at the wrong time." Do you see how backward that is? The customer was at the right place at the right time. The customer was doing what he was supposed to be doing. It was the psycho with the gun who was at the wrong place at the wrong time!

I want to tell you that *it is not God's fault!* We're always quick to blame God, but it's not God's fault. I want to show you that there is no possible way to appreciate the life of God and the forgiveness of God unless you see what life is like without God's light. I could discuss words like *grace*, *redemption*, *forgiveness*, and *salvation*. But there is no way to fully appreciate these words until you know what life looks like without the character of Christ in it.

A life without character, a life without the life of Christ in it, is capable of anything. That is exactly what Paul is writing about in Romans 1. He's answering these questions: Why is there so much evil? Why is there so much suffering? How is it that people can do things like that to each other? If it's not God's fault, then how could all of this be happening?

Evil Experienced

We All Have Dead Spirits

> *For the wrath of God is revealed from heaven against all ungodliness and unrighteousness of men who suppress the truth in unrighteousness*. (Romans 1:18)

After Satan talked Eve into giving up her God-given responsibility to "Edenize" the planet, I'm sure Adam thought, *Okay, God. Eve blew it, but I've got another rib. Just put me to sleep, and I'll take a do over.* But with their own free will, both Adam and Eve chose to side not with God but with the enemy and all of his cohorts. This was like a cosmic game of "Red Rover." The enemy called out, "Come on over." Adam and Eve took off in a sprint, and the enemy said, "We got you!" When the enemy trapped Adam and Eve, they broke fellowship with God, and their spirits died.

Most of my friends are married, and they've been married long enough to have kids. They always call and say, "You've got to come see the baby! Come see it!"

I usually respond, "I don't have to come see the baby. I'm single; I've got no responsibility."

Without missing a beat they counter my rebuttal: "No, you've got to come see the baby. Come see the baby." So I give in and go see the baby.

Now, I'm single, and I know nothing about kids. You could put a dog and a baby side by side, and I would not be able to tell them apart. I wouldn't know! I'm out of that whole world.

When I get over to the house, the parents hijack me for a compliment: "Isn't he the cutest thing you've ever seen?"

I ask them, "Are you willing to put our friendship on the line for the sake of a compliment?"

They just smile and wait for my compliment.

"Well, he certainly has a large head. He's got his own little atmosphere rotating around it. Out of all of the babies that I've ever seen, he is one of them."

They say, "Isn't he the cutest thing you've ever seen?"

On the inside I want to go, "No, he's not! His ears don't really fit his head. His knuckles drag the ground. You've basically got a monkey. You've just given birth to a monkey! Look at that!" All of us know couples that just should not procreate. I'm not judging; I'm just saying that if you have to get a license to fish, shouldn't you have to have one to start a family?

They say, "He's got his father's eyes. He's got his mother's head. He's got his mother's lips."

I can sort of see the resemblance. If I step back I can say, "From a distance he sort of looks like Mussolini; but up close, I can see it."

The government and well-meaning teachers can say, "All mankind is basically good." But we're not. At the core of who we really are, there is no basic good. We're bad because we have dead spirits. That is why all of these horrible things are happening in our world. People with dead spirits do dead things. They act in line with the way they are inside. They are dead spiritually. This is why Paul says that we *"all have sinned and fall short"* (Romans 3:23). We all have missed the mark.

Those of us who've grown up in the church with both of our parents at home have missed the mark. Those of us who've had everything stacked against us since childhood have missed the mark. This is why Paul is clear to say that *"there is none righteous"* (Romans 3:10). *"There is none who does good"* (Romans 3:12). It could not be any clearer.

We Experience a Denial of Salvation

> *That which is known about God is evident within them; for God made it evident to them. For since the creation of the*

> *world His invisible attributes, His eternal power and divine nature, have been clearly seen, being understood through what has been made, so that they are without excuse.* (Romans 1:19–20)

God makes sure that everyone in the world is faced with the reality of his or her sin and need of God's life through Jesus Christ. It doesn't matter where people are; God takes care of getting the message of Christ to them. Just remember, God communicates with man in many different ways. He is not limited in the ways He communicates.

Read the reports of the guys that kill their classmates at school, and what you find is that several of them had some kind of exposure to a church. Imagine for a moment that one of these students attended a youth service once where a speaker talked about the life of Christ, His death on the cross, and His resurrection. The speaker closed the talk with an invitation, asking if anybody wanted to ask Christ to come into his or her heart. Having heard the message, that person turned the invitation down. Each person can reject or receive God. Each of us has the ability to choose.

At some point in life everyone is offered the hope and life of Jesus Christ. When this offer is refused, that denial—added to a negative family background plus a lot of anger, angst, and rage—makes that human capable of almost anything.

This is why it's impossible for somebody to say, "Well, I didn't know." Paul is saying, "Even if you didn't hear it, you were created on the inside to know that there is something missing, so you are without excuse."

One of the great stoner questions I get asked is, "How many angels can sit on the head of a pin?" I want to respond, "If Jesus was a Jew, then why the Spanish name?"

A more serious question people ask is, "What about the people who never hear about Jesus?" Paul addresses that. All people come into this world knowing that something is missing and sensing that there is Someone who gave them life. Even if they don't know what to call this life force, they still have the opportunity to receive or reject it. Everybody around the globe is without excuse. They have sensed it, they have heard it, or they have seen it in creation. They've seen it in the water, in the stars, or in the trees and flowers. The Bible is very clear that all creation was fashioned to point toward the reality and presence of God. We are all without excuse.

People are amazed when somebody does something unpredictable. There was a guy in Atlanta who went into his office building and killed twenty people because he didn't get a raise. When his coworkers were interviewed, they all said the same thing: "We didn't really know him very well; he was kind of a quiet guy." Why should that surprise anyone? If you're a mass killer, you don't have business cards printed up. Mass killers don't post an instant message saying, "Hi, I'm going to unload the clip in the office tomorrow." They don't post listings on the bulletin board: "E-mail me if you need anybody killed." They're supposed to be quiet; they're supposed to be reserved. They're psycho!

All mankind has a dead spirit. God shows everyone that they can trade their dead spirits for His live one, but many decline the invitation.

It Begins a Downward Spiral

In the passage that follows, notice the outline of the downward spiral that happens when a person rejects God's offer: (a) darkened heart; (b) degrading passions; (c) depraved mind. Each cycle of the spiral leads to a lower level that is more destructive than the last.

> *For even though they knew God, they did not honor Him as God or give thanks, but they became futile in their speculations, and their foolish* heart was darkened. *Professing to be wise, they became fools, and exchanged the glory of the incorruptible God for an image in the form of corruptible man and of birds and four-footed animals and crawling creatures. Therefore God gave them over in the lusts of their hearts.... For they exchanged the truth of God for a lie, and worshiped and served the creature rather than the Creator.... God gave them over to* degrading passions....

> *God gave them over to a* depraved mind. (Romans 1: 21–26, 28)

Darkened Heart

> *Their foolish heart was darkened.... Therefore God gave them over in the lusts of their hearts.* (Romans 1:21, 24)

These people reject the light that is revealed to them. That light is "*the Light of men,*" and the darkness rejects it (John 1:4–5). They reject the offer of the life of Jesus Christ. Now the darkness that they were familiar with becomes the basis for their entire reality.

Perhaps we find it difficult to understand why anyone would willingly exchange the light of God's life for a life of corruption. Perhaps, too, we can understand that a darkened heart is the natural consequence when a person chooses rejection of Christ as the final answer.

Degrading Passions

> *For this reason God gave them over to degrading passions.* (Romans 1:26)

Rejecting the life of God begins to skew passions. It results in a hunger for horrible things and a craving for things that are not proper or right. Things that once were unthinkable become topics of interest and curiosity. The evil living in their darkened heart becomes their companion and trusted friend. What once was horribly wrong is now justifiable considering their circumstances. Choices and actions that were once completely unacceptable are now clearly understandable because "that's just how things work out sometimes." Life's choices are not based on right and wrong; they are based on what feels right. Rules—any rule—can be changed. If feeling bad about what they're doing is removed, then they don't have to control their behavior.

Depraved Mind

> *God gave them over to a depraved mind, to do those things which are not proper.* (Romans 1:28)

Next they begin to live out their degraded passions. With a darkened heart and degraded passions, that darkness festers inside of them. Just as yeast in bread dough expands to permeate every part of the loaf, the darkness sooner or later permeates every part of their lives. And God gives them over to this darkness.

Guns don't kill people, the person pulling the trigger does. The music or the movie is not what causes some people to choose evil actions. The music and the movie are the gasoline that is thrown on a dead spirit with evil passions. It's easy to judge the medium and miss the motivator. Destroy all the CDs you want, and still the darkened spirit is not impacted. It is the dead spirit and evil passions that use the music or the movie to justify the actions they have already chosen to take.

Not everyone makes it all the way down this spiral. You can stop it. You can break the cycle. But that's the focus of chapter 3.

We Become Capable of Despicable Sins

> *God gave them over to a depraved mind, to do those things which are not proper, being filled with all unrighteousness, wickedness, greed, evil; full of envy, murder, strife, deceit, malice; they are gossips, slanderers, haters of* God*, insolent, arrogant, boastful, inventors of evil, disobedient to parents, without understanding, untrustworthy, unloving, unmerciful.* (Romans 1:28–31)

At first glance the preceding list seems to be a random listing of sins. This list is all the depraved character that man is capable of producing. It all originates and finds motivation out of a darkened heart. A darkened heart leads to degrading passions, which lead to a depraved mind. The natural outflow of this type of life is despicable sins. Here is what you need to know: *People with dead spirits do dead things.*

Paul lays out a list of despicable sins. It's not music; it's not TV. It's not the fault of white hats or trench coats. The guys who killed their schoolmates at Columbine used the excuse that they didn't have any friends! If you saw the news, then you saw that there were six of them in their group. I didn't have six friends my whole six years of high school. Six friends are enough to put together a basketball team. Six people aren't enough friends?

Speculations were flying through the air: "It was their parents. It was their black trench coats. It was the Goth-rock." How about the fact that there was something wrong inside them? How about the fact that they had dead spirits; they turned down the offer for the life of Christ? How about the fact that they engaged in a downward spiral that began to play itself out in their actions, and they were capable of doing anything despicable?

Let's not marginalize this whole issue by pointing at entertainment and radio and politics and parents. The issue of character is not the improvement of humanity. The issue of character is not making people better. The issue is that we have something innately wrong in us that must be fixed.

The frightening thought that occurred to me as I read this passage in Romans 1 is that if our foundation were ripped away, any one of us would be capable of doing the same thing the Columbine students did. Left to ourselves, every one of us has a tremendous capacity for evil. Something has got to be fixed. Being moral won't fix it. Having better church attendance won't fix it. Being religious won't fix it.

Our society has been taught that people evolved from amoebas, fish, and monkeys. Evolution is about the survival of the fittest. Let me tell you how this translates in the mind of the average high-school student: *Whoever has the biggest gun wins*. Morality won't fix this. A curriculum change won't make much difference. As good as church is, just showing up on Sundays won't fix it.

There is no way to appreciate the life of God until you have seen what life looks like without it. Many of us have not only seen it, we have lived it. And unless something is done and done quickly, we will live out the rest of our lives having the finality of death as our only hope.

See one area of your life as God's garden. It can be a relationship or situation at home or at work. Find several specific ways to "Edenize" this relationship or situation. The focus is to bring the presence of God back into or further into it.

THREE

Live Lights

GOD'S PLAN FOR GETTING OUT OF THE DARKNESS

Not long ago I boarded a single-engine plane with a friend of mine who was the pilot. The only people who die in these kinds of planes are famous rock stars or politicians, and since I am neither, I have no fear of flying in them.

I was scheduled to speak early Sunday morning in Kentucky, so in order to make it to the first service, we took off from Oklahoma City at about two o'clock in the morning. The plan was to fly to a halfway point to refuel and then complete the journey to our final destination. If all went as planned, we would make it to the airport in Kentucky, and I'd have forty minutes to get to church.

A storm moved in on the airport, however, making our final approach quite turbulent. The plane's wipers flapped madly at the rain, but visibility remained poor. The wind tossed the plane, and my friend fought to hold on to the steering wheel. He was flying completely by instinct; there wasn't time to think about reacting to the wind's violent changes. Up, down, left, right, twisting, falling, rising—the plane was being thrown like a small boat in a perfect storm.

Now my friend was steering with one hand and pulling out maps with the other. His feet and hands moved quickly and accurately to keep the plane as stable as possible. *Why is he reading at a time like this?* I thought to myself. *This is no time to read.*

I had never heard a plane groan, but this one did. It shook and made sounds that made me want to lose my stomach. Looking out the window for something stable, all I could see was fog. A thick blanket had covered the airport. The landing strip was below us…somewhere.

I looked at my friend, who was doing a lousy job of hiding his concern. "If we make this landing," he said, "it will be an absolute miracle. And if this weather doesn't change, we won't be able to land." I didn't know what to say. I couldn't say anything anyway; fear had dried out my mouth. My tongue and my jaw would not move.

The instrumentation on the plane told us the airport was there, but we couldn't see it. Our eyes worked fine, but between the fog and the rain we couldn't see it. Pilots know that in these situations you don't trust your eyes; you trust your instruments.

We descended into clouds and fog that moved like cream poured into coffee. A voice from the airport tower barked out orders, and my friend maneuvered the plane so that the instruments matched what he was being told. Everything inside me said, *Pull up. Don't go down there! I don't see safety there. I really don't trust what I can't see.*

It was as if my friend heard me screaming these things in my head. He turned to me and spoke through a half smile, "We're not going to crash. You will get to preach this morning." I returned the smile, although mine was a bit shaky. "See," I said to him, "I told you I wasn't famous." We both laughed.

I'm not a pilot, but I fly almost every day. I've been in storms, but not often ones like this one. I guess the fact that I was there with the pilot in the cockpit made the reality of the situation all the more clear. I heard the man in the tower telling us to descend. I saw the numbers on the altimeter falling. I felt every time the wind hit the side of the plane. I saw the concern on my friend's face. I felt the fear.

Then the plane dipped wildly, almost out of control. The pilot's hands compensated, and we braced for the worst. But the worst had passed. Just below us, exactly in our path, the clouds began to thin and then to split as if pointing the way. Our eyes adjusted, and we saw the blue lights of the runway. That long line of blue lights lit the way to safety.

There is a fog that clouds the hearts of men like a dense mist, and the enemy places it there. This covering is the condition of all those who have darkened hearts. This darkness brings trouble from within the hearts of the human race. It is denser and more foreboding than any fog a plane flies through. And there is only one thing that can remove this fog.

Just as the change of wind blows away the fog and the morning sun burns away the mist, the breath of God and the light of Christ's life remove the darkness that covers men's hearts. The dark world looks for a place of safety but sees none. The light and life of Christ is their only hope for a safe landing.

The apostle Paul tells us that God has given us the Spirit of God "*so that we may know the things freely given to us by God*" (1 Corinthians 2:12). We are able to know the life of God because He has blown away the clouds and taken away the power of darkness.

The *lit* life begins with salvation. Salvation is the life of God living in us...and that is character. Some think of character as a kind of life or a lifestyle. Character far exceeds that. Character is God's own life coming to live in us.

Not long ago I ate with a friend of mine at the golf and country club where he is a member. (I gave up golf when I realized I couldn't get the ball past the windmill.) When the bill came, the waiter placed it in front of me. My friend said, "Just put it on my tab." Spiritually, this is what happens as well. My darkened heart was placed on Jesus' tab. He paid for my evil nature. One character was exchanged for another.

The Old Testament is written in Hebrew, and when the word *salvation* is used, it is in a military context. It literally means to win over darkness. It also means to have victory over evil, to seize the enemy and overcome him.

Salvation is a big, churchy word, and it can be dangerous to use it with postmoderns. It's a theological word and can be hard to understand. But because it does have a great deal of significance, I want you to understand what it means.

We tend to think of salvation in a very one-dimensional way: praying a prayer, checking a box, walking an aisle, agreeing with a pastor about some things that he says, attending a class or two, and then getting sprinkled or dunked. For most of us it means that after death we get to go to heaven and miss all the unpleasant things about going to hell, where you end up smelling worse than a burned toaster pastry. This is pretty much how a lot of us would define salvation. It's something we do to secure something later on, after our lives end. But understanding salvation the way God understands it brings both the future elements and the here-and-now elements together. Salvation is just as much about the present as it is about the future.

Salvation is the cosmic plan of God for bringing light into our darkened world. This plan is the only hope we have to become living lights that overcome the darkness.

First Peter is a great little book in the New Testament. Six verses from this book will help you see just how God plans on re-creating you into a living light.

It Is Predicted

> *As to this salvation, the prophets who prophesied of the grace that would come to you made careful searches and inquiries.*
> (1 Peter 1:10)

Salvation is not a new concept. It did not begin in this century, it didn't begin with televangelists, and it didn't begin with organized religion. Salvation began in the Garden of Eden. After Adam and Eve chose sides with the cosmic Mafia, God said to the enemy, "I am going to send My Son, who is going to crush your head." That was the promise of salvation. Jesus would come and ultimately crush the power that Satan had over the world and mankind.

The other day someone challenged me after I spoke. "Christianity is not the oldest religion," the person said. "There are others that are older, and Christianity is a version of those." Well, let's see. The first reference to Christianity was in the Garden of Eden after the Fall

(Genesis 3:15). How much older does it have to be? Since the beginning of time, God has been doing one thing: He has been moving and overtaking darkness to bring salvation to people.

The biblical record of salvation was continued throughout the Old Testament as the prophets wrote and told the people what God was going to do. The story of the Old Testament is salvation. It is the story of God rescuing Israel from the darkness of Pharaoh's army. It is the account of God providing for all their needs while they made their journey to the Promised Land. The Old Testament is the salvation story. That picture helps us understand how God works in our lives. He comes to the point where we are caught by the darkness, and He rescues us.

Through the Spirit of God, the prophets saw the future light that God would provide in Christ. Their vision of the light overcoming the darkness and the inability of the darkness to conquer the light was clear. They spoke of salvation in terms of a promise made by God that He would one day place His Spirit inside His people. God would no longer live in a gold-covered box behind a curtain; He would live in people. Through this new covenant, God would sacrifice His Son and remove sin, forgive people, set them free, and place His spirit inside them.

All of history has been about this one word: *salvation*. Listen to what Malachi 3:1 says: "*Behold, I am going to send My messenger, and he will clear the way before Me. And the Lord, whom you seek, will suddenly come to His temple; and the messenger of the covenant, in whom you delight, behold, He is coming.*" The prophets predicted that Jesus was coming. Jeremiah predicted what He was going to do. Isaiah laid it out in crystal-clear detail, and then Jesus came and fulfilled all of these predictions. God did not have to come up with a new plan. His plan has been steadily worked out throughout history.

Christ's coming fulfilled the prophecy spoken in Isaiah 9:2: "*The people who walk in darkness will see a great light.*" This is the explicit description of the human race. They once were walking in darkness, trying to find their way out, but could not. To make matters worse, in their futile search for a way out of the darkness, their hearts became cynical. But Christ came as the one great light from God.

Jeremiah 31:33–34 says, "*I will put My law within them and on their heart I will write it; and I will be their God, and they shall be My people.... For I will forgive their iniquity, and their sin I will remember no more.*" All the promises God made to mankind in the Old Testament recognized and pointed to the new covenant of God coming to live in man. No longer would man and God be separated, but God's Spirit would actually cohabit with man's spirit. He would make man's heart His home. He would be in a complete relationship with him. The union would be so complete, so perfect, that God would no longer remember the sin.

Ezekiel 36:26 puts it this way: "*I will give you a new heart and put a new spirit within you; and I will remove the heart of stone from your flesh and give you a heart of flesh.*" When God comes to cohabitate within the heart of a man, He re-creates that man into someone he was not before. He places within that man a new heart. He places within him the light of life. From the inside out, that man becomes a living light.

What God set in motion way back at the beginning of the world, He did so that He could work in you. Think of it. God created the world. He placed the prophets in specific places so they could see the coming ministry and life of Jesus. Jesus came and defeated the cosmic Mafia, defeated the godfather on his own turf, by his own terms. God has been actively at work throughout history so that He can live in you and me. This is the radical message of salvation.

It Is Practical

> *Therefore, prepare your minds for action, keep sober in spirit, fix your hope completely on...Jesus Christ.* (1 Peter 1:13)

It is not just a prayer that you pray. It is not just a phrase that you say. It's not just a game you play. (I am starting to rhyme...do you hear what I say?) Salvation has practical outcomes in our lives. It affects us in practical ways. How much more practical can you get than your mind, your spirit, and your hope?

"*Therefore, prepare your minds.*" Peter lets us know that salvation affects our thought life. Someone once said that we ultimately become what we think about most. The most dominant thought in the human mind is self. If our most dominant thought only reinforces the deadness that lives in us, we are in deep trouble.

Salvation changes the dark to light. It re-creates the dead life into live light. Because it takes place on the inside, it is possible to change the way we think of ourselves.

God knows who we are. We each embark on this spiritual journey as different people with different quirks and bents in our lives. God knows that some of our parents were Ozzie and Harriet, and some of them were just horrible. He even knows that some of us are still angry with them. (Hey, your parents' job was to prepare you for life by messing with your mind and your emotions. They did their job; now leave them alone. Let it go...please.) God understands it all, and He gets you.

Each of us chooses one of four roles in life that we hope will bring us the security, love, and comfort we require in relationships. Sometime in about our junior-high or high-school years we pick a role that we end up playing for life. See which of these roles you have chosen. The idea here is not to cause you pain but to give you personal insight into your life as you seek to live *lit*.

1. *"I am going to please people so they will love me."* People who choose this role become successful, make great grades, and do well in life. They might have been cheerleaders or football players. They always smell like vanilla; they have good auras. They sit at the right lunch tables, they have beautiful friends, and lunchtime looks like a live Abercrombie ad. These are the pleasers. Every one is cut and chiseled and ripped with developed six packs (while I just have a two-liter). The pleasers say, "I am going to please people so they will notice me and love me."

2. *"I am going to become a problem so people will notice me."* Some people grow up challenging every rule and presence of authority. They become the exact opposite of Mom and Dad. They go out and take all kinds of risks and make all sorts of hurtful choices.

Problem people say, "I am going to do everything they don't want me to do. I am going to be a huge problem just so people will notice me." It all boils down to people noticing them. These people just decide to become someone who constantly stirs up trouble and cuts against the grain. Their only motivation is to tick people off and get the attention they crave.

3. *"I am going to take care of people so they will need me."* These are the people who become the parents of everyone, even their friends. They take care of everyone's emotions and everyone's needs. These people grow up and become teachers or take on some other kind of nurturing role. They are the nurturers in their relationships and in their families, and they become providers just so people will love them.
4. *"I am going to withdraw from people so they will leave me alone."* These people become recluses. They stay in their rooms, and the only people they meet are on the Internet. The Internet has always been kind of shady. You meet people who introduce themselves by "handles." A person tells you her name is "Sexy X" or something like that. You think she sounds beautiful, but you're really in a chat room with a four-hundred-pound cross-country truck driver named Tiny.

The point is this: God understands you, and He understands why you do what you do. No matter what your life looks like, God gets you. There is no life so messed up that He can't make all good. Whatever you do for a living, whomever you have chosen to hang out with, the hobbies you have chosen, the music you prefer, the places you go, the values you keep, and the decisions you make—all come out of the life role that you play.

God created your humanity. He knows who you are physically, psychologically, and emotionally. He made your personality. Nothing is happening in your life today that is going to shock God, because He understands you.

God meets you where you are in the role you have chosen. That role will lead you into situations that will literally bring you face to face with what God wants to do in your life. God is so in tune with who you are that He is able to take you and your role and change both from the inside out. It is impossible to experience salvation and not be changed at a practical level.

It's a Process

For you have been born again not of seed which is perishable but imperishable. (1 Peter 1:23)

If we are not careful how we present salvation, a person could believe that salvation is just a matter of presenting facts and getting someone to believe them. Granted, the facts must never be neglected, but the dark problem within mankind cannot be solved with facts. The Spirit of God must process a work in each person.

Just as a seed has growth phases, there are three distinct parts to salvation. These three cannot truly be separated and, therefore, should be viewed as a whole.

The first is *conviction*. Without conviction, no one can come to Christ. We cannot come to Christ on our own terms in our time, when we are good and ready. John 16:8 tells us it is the *Holy Spirit* who convicts.

Conviction usually manifests itself as guilt over the past or dissatisfaction with the present. Conviction is something you can feel physically. It's a kind of tightness that comes over you. This is not a bad feeling; it's God's way of drawing us to Him. "*No one can come to Me unless the Father who sent Me draws him*" (John 6:44).

Our brains are not the source of life; the Holy Spirit is. It is entirely possible to hear the truth and still have a hardened heart. It is the Holy Spirit who brings salvation, not the mind, and it's not our own desire. Salvation comes completely from God.

The second part of salvation is *choice*. In this part, we first have to believe in who Jesus is. This is more than agreeing with what the Bible says about Jesus. It is literally placing our full dependence for all of life in who Jesus is—believing *into* who Jesus is. Believing into Jesus is a personal reliance on the person and character of Christ. Then, we must repent, which means to move away *from* something and *toward* something completely different. Finally, we must receive. This is our choice. We sense the Holy Spirit erupting in us, and we hear our hearts saying, "It's true! You can believe it!" We realize we are separated from God, and we surrender fully to Him. Anything less than this is not salvation. There must be a moment of clear choice, and the choice must be made out of conviction.

The third part of salvation is *conversion*. Ephesians 2:1 says, "*You were dead in your trespasses and sins*." That's why the things of God were lifeless to us. Our sins made us dead to the things of God. When the speaker gave the invitation, it was death that kept us in our seats.

As bearers of the light, we must be careful not to reduce the process of salvation to a formula. I hear preachers all the time who reduce salvation almost to a drive-through speaker interface. They lead people through quick-menu prayer selections as if they were offering the big burger combo number four.

The Spirit of God must initiate the salvation process. It's more than just trusting that the number four you ordered will be prepared to order when you drive up to the window.

Anne Lamott, in her book *Traveling Mercies: Some Thoughts on Faith*, tells her story of conversion. It is one of the most honest and authentic that I have come across in quite a while. She begins by telling how her life had intersected with a small church, a congregation of people who lived an authentic and observable faith in Christ. She would visit this church once a month.

As she tells it, "It was the singing that pulled me in and split me wide open. Something inside of me that was stiff and rotting would feel soft and tender. Somehow the singing wore down all the boundaries and distinctions that kept me so isolated."

That April of 1984, she found out she was pregnant. She didn't have the money or the wherewithal to have a baby. The father was someone she had just met, and he was married. He was not someone she wanted to have a baby or a life with. So one evening her friend Pammy took her to get an abortion. Later that night Pammy brought her home, and Anne went upstairs to her loft with a pint of liquor and some of the codeine a nurse had given her for pain. She drank until nearly dawn. Her life went on that way for a week.

She writes, "I stayed at home and smoked dope and got drunk and tried to write a little. I got into bed shaky and too wild to have another drink or take a sleeping pill. I had a cigarette and turned off the light. I became aware of someone with me. Hunkered down in the corner. The feeling was so strong I actually turned on the light for a moment to make sure no one was there—of course there wasn't. But after a while in the dark again, I knew beyond any doubt that it was Jesus. I felt Him just sitting there on His haunches in the corner of my sleeping loft watching me with patience and love. I squinted my eyes shut, but that did not help, because that was not what I was seeing Him with. Finally I fell asleep, and in the morning He was gone…

"One week later I went back to church. I was so hung over I could not stand up for the songs. I began to cry and left before the benediction and raced home. I opened the door to my houseboat and stood there for a minute. Then I hung my head and said, 'I quit.' I took a long deep breath and said out loud, 'All right. You can come in.'"[1]

If the pastor of the church Anne Lamott attended had tried some heavy-handed salvation closer on her, that moment may have been lost. Salvation is a process for every individual. Anne had to come to God in her own way through her own life role and in the timing when God was ready to truly reach her. She prayed her own prayer in her own words, but it was at the conviction and invitation of the Spirit of God.

It Produces

As obedient children… (1 Peter 1:14)

The salvation God brings into our lives produces three things in us.

1. New Family

I know people whose hobby is tracing their genealogies. Many of them have found that their family tree has more offshoots and veins than a weightlifter's thighs. I also know people whose family tree I suspect was a wreath. (Let's just move on.) Then there's me. I come from a small family. Basically, my family tree is a twig. The point of all of this is that at the moment we receive the light of God, we are taken out of one family tree and placed into the family of God.

Up to the point of salvation, we were in the family of darkness. Jesus Himself made this distinction. He saw the heritage of every person living without light as coming from the devil. In John 8:44 He said, "*You are of your father the devil.*"

When we are made into living light, we become members of the family of light. Darkness no longer has a hold on us. We live in the family of God.

2. Absolute Forgiveness

What separated us from God was not lying, cheating, stealing, or killing. It was our sin nature, our sin character. Because of Christ, the old character has been done away with. The new character, the character of Christ, has come into our lives. The forgiveness we have received is not partial; it is not contingent on our future behavior. It is the absolute removal of darkness.

This is what Paul is trying to get his readers to see in Romans 8:31 when he writes, "*If God is for us, who is against us?*" The answer is no one! Paul asks again in verse 33, "*Who will bring a charge against God's elect?*" The answer is no one, not even the devil himself. Because of personal salvation, we become untouchable by our mistakes. No one can hold our sins against us when they are covered by Christ's blood.

Many of us struggle with the past in the present because we don't know how forgiven we really are. Every mistake, failure, and sin has been removed so that we are free to face life with confidence.

3. Total Freedom

All traces of darkness can be overcome in our lives because Christ has overcome the evil one. If that's true, then why all the personal struggles?

Sometimes in hostage situations, the ones who have been taken hostage become sympathetic with their captors. When they are told they are no longer captives and are free, they want to stay. The same thing happens to us spiritually. Every time evil wins in our lives, it is because we return back to our captor when we really are free. We are free from sin and free from the evil one. Because of this personal salvation, we have become children of light.

As obedient children, the life of Christ has now been placed in our lives. This character of Christ, this light, comes in and begins to ignite our lives. Only God can do these things. That is why Isaiah 53:5 says, "*By His scourging [wounds] we are healed.*" That promise is not limited to physical healing but is a salvation verse. By His wounds we were made again. By His work on the cross and our dependence on Him, we were made over.

Christianity, however, says you and I can't do any of this unless Christ does something in us. We don't have it in us to act like Christ. So He has to come in and produce that ability to surrender, submit, and serve.

It's Personal

> *...obtaining as the outcome of your faith the salvation of your souls.* (1 Peter 1:9)

We must use our will that God has given us to make the choice of salvation. He will not force it on us, nor will He trick us into receiving His gift. He gives the gift of His life only to those who exercise their will and request Him to come and inhabit their lives.

Living *lit* requires us to drop our guard, open our lives, and admit, "God, I can't live this *lit* life, but you can." It starts with a prayer like, "God, I can't do this anymore. I can't do this out of my own strength; I don't have it in me. Would you please step out of heaven and step into my heart?"

If you have never connected with the life of Christ—even if you've been in church your whole life, but there was never a genuine moment—would you pray this prayer?

Take a moment and write your own prayer of surrender.

It's Purposeful

> *...to obtain an inheritance which is imperishable and undefiled and will not fade away.* (1 Peter 1:4)

The good news of the bad news is that what was lost in the Garden is returned at salvation. Man gets it all back, and it's not going away.

In the Garden, man stepped out of light and into darkness. In salvation, man is stepping out of darkness and into light. Salvation is getting out of your old character and taking on the new character of Christ.

God has a purpose for this light within you that is greater than you have ever imagined. Salvation is not just about heaven. It is about your understanding and living out your God-given destiny on this earth.

Place a small sign on your mirror (or somewhere you can see it) that says, "Recognize your new self." When you look at your reflection each morning, form an intention to spend the rest of the day observing your words and actions so that you might eliminate those that are harmful to yourself and others. Focus on the character of Christ living in you. And when you see yourself in the mirror, know that you are seeing a reflection of God's light as it is manifest in you.

FOUR

Get *Lit*

WHAT GOD DOES *TO* US HE DOES *THROUGH* US

The Christmas story is all about God reaching down to man just when he needs Him the most.

Christmastime. Stockings, hot apple cider, carols, wreaths, and unshaven men ringing bells outside of the mall. I'm on my way to the mall to buy some Christmas gifts for my friends and relatives, and the wind nearly blows the list out of my glove-covered hand. If it weren't for the sticky coating on one edge, the small yellow square might have gotten away.

I usually enjoy shopping, but not at this time of year. The Bible says to treat others the way you want them to treat you. Well, I tried that three years ago and bought some really nice gifts for three friends. One of them finally gave me a Christmas card last week. It had a bookstore gift certificate in it, and he told me through as sincere a grin as I have ever seen, "Hey man, don't spend it all in one place." I looked at the slip of paper. It was a *gift certificate*. How could I not spend it all in one place? I looked a bit closer and saw that it had expired three months before. The second friend forgot me altogether, and the third—well, the third actually gave me something I can use...matching oven mitts.

People tell me that it's not the gift that matters, it's the thought. All I've got to say is, someone's not thinking enough.

I was thinking the other day about this whole Christmas thing. Santa is spelled with the same letters as Satan, just in a different order. Santa works only one week a year; Satan works year-round. Satan is able to keep up that pace only because he isn't married. Both of these guys wear red, both of them work at night, but one is real and one is not. And of course you know which one I mean.

I never have understood the traditional Christmas drink, eggnog. I know what an egg is, but exactly what is a person drinking when he is drinking a *nog?* I've never actually tasted eggnog; I can't seem to get beyond the thickness of it. It has the consistency of white school glue and looks like it could be used to patch a hole in the wall. Who came up with the idea of combining eggs and alcohol anyway? I've heard of beer and pretzels, wine and cheese—but eggs and alcohol? And why at Christmastime is it festive to drink eggs and alcohol? Aren't eggs an Easter thing? By the way, I wouldn't recommend using eggnog to patch a wall. I'm no expert, but the alcohol might keep the patch from passing code inspection.

Getting *lit* is what the Christmas story in Luke 2 is all about—the world being *lit* with the presence of God. We see firsthand that when Christ came to this earth, God was breaking into human history to establish His rule on earth and defeat darkness.

Just as Jesus came into this world born among the common things of life, He spent the next thirty-three years of His life harassed firsthand by the daily struggles of humanity. But this would not be the last time that God would live among the people. What God was doing through Christ, He is now doing through us. We function as the light of God on the earth.

The Other Side of Salvation

The cross is not just about us. To emphasize only its personal benefits is to undersell its value, meaning, and impact on the world. "*For God so loved the world, that He gave His only begotten Son....*" (John 3:16). The death of Christ impacted the entire universe. The battle that was started by the cosmic Mafia was ended at the cross. Christ recaptured His rightful rule over the entire cosmos.

The enemy had taken the world and captured mankind; with His death, Christ defeated the enemy and his mob. His victory at the cross destroyed their power to keep people in darkness. The power is broken, but the presence of darkness still remains. There is still plenty of work to be done.

The cross not only defeated the power of the enemy; it also began to establish the kingdom of God on earth. As Christians we have a place in Christ's universal win, but we seem to have lost sight of our role in extending His earthly kingdom. Perhaps we never knew it. Salvation makes us ready to serve the greater purpose of God by defeating the enemy and making that defeat visible in this world.

At the moment of salvation, we receive a new nature. We are taken out of darkness and placed in the light. We are prepared to live as Jesus lived while on this earth. We who were once ruled by the cosmic Mafia are now the ones who work with God to destroy it. As bearers of His presence, we extend to our generation the invitation to come out of darkness and live in the light.

In one of the opening scenes of the movie *Gladiator*, Russell Crowe's character turns to his army and says, "What we do here will echo in eternity." As you and I are ignited by God's presence, our deeds truly will fulfill His eternal purpose. What we do will echo for eternity.

Salvation is what God does in us and through us. Bringing the presence of His kingdom to our world is what God does through His believers. He does this first through personal salvation and then by sending out His light through our works. Each generation must find the most effective ways to demonstrate God's presence within its culture.

Finding New Language in Old Words

Language is a funny thing. I spent a week in Brussels and ate some sprouts. Then I went to Belgium and had a waffle. Tasty. While in both places I had to deal with the language barrier. It wasn't that I had forgotten how to speak; it was that the sounds of my words made no sense to the people trying to get me food. Since yelling in English didn't work, I resorted to ordering by picture and pointing to the combo number by the big smiling clown. I was glad to get back to the States, where I could get incompetent service in a language I could understand.

Old, churchy words sometimes mean absolutely nothing to us. We hear them and just give one of those crooked-smiling, head-nodding, one-eyebrow-raised, act-like-I-know-it "oh yeah's." It's like doing a card trick for a dog. It just doesn't connect. The dog cocks its head as you tell it to pick a card. It raises its ears just a bit and wonders how it's supposed to pick a card without any thumbs.

In this chapter I want to take some old, important, churchy words and give you some really good stuff to help you understand the new language that is hidden in these old terms. When we speak about the presence of God, don't focus on the words about His presence; focus on what the words signify. The words are just the tip of the iceberg. They point to the light and the change that the presence of God brings to our lives.

One of the mistakes believers make today is to believe that simply saying words brings about the change. We say, "I have been inhabited by the incarnate, resurrected, glorified, omnipotent Christ. He is in the process of sanctifying my life and bringing His priceless redemption fully to bear on the world around me." Every time I hear something like this, I tilt my head and thank God I do have thumbs.

If we are to live *lit* lives, we must understand the meaning within the meaning of these words. We must recognize that our call is to live more of our lives as a light in the darkness than as just another light in an already lighted sanctuary. In his book *Letters and Papers from Prison*, Dietrich Bonhoeffer says, "Our church, which has been fighting in these years only for its self-preservation, as though that were an end in itself, is incapable of taking the work of reconciliation and redemption to mankind and the world."[1] If the people in darkness are going to recognize light when they see it, we must understand the process of change

God is working in us and allow the light of Christ to shine in and through everything we do.

In this section we will go back to the old words in order to extract from them our *lit* language. Four words in particular show us clearly that what God has done *to* us, He now desires to do *through* us. These four words—incarnation, reconciliation, supernatural, and glorification—are exposed in Luke 2, when God invaded the world.

1. *Incarnation* Increases Light

> God has become flesh: *"For today in the city of David there has been born for you a Savior, who is Christ the Lord."* (Luke 2:11)

God's coming into the world in the form of a baby is a radical concept to many. All around the world, the images of Joseph, Mary, the baby, the animals, the shepherds, and the wise men are mainstays for Christmas decorations. But few have ever stopped to think about the fact that God chose to take on human flesh and wait it out inside of Mary for nine months. He voluntarily chose to enter this world through the birth canal and limit His abilities and experiences to that of every other infant—messy diapers, breast-feeding, the total incapacity for taking care of Himself. He had to learn to talk and run and climb a tree. He had to learn how to control every one of His newly discovered human abilities. This was Jesus' coming into this world.

In John 1:14 the original manuscripts say that Jesus "skinned" among us. That means that He put on skin and lived in our midst. This is God's taking on the form of Jesus and breaking into human history to defeat darkness and to establish the righteousness of God.

Incarnation is God's connecting to the world. It is His coming in human form to legally take back His creation. It is God's making our interests His interests. God links arms with us and our problems, and He walks through the blood, the tears, the spit, and the stories of our lives.

When we give our lives to Christ, we receive Him. He becomes "skinned" in our lives. We are incarnations of Christ. We become sons and daughters of God. That means we are carrying inside of us the presence that is greater than every fear we will ever face. The presence that is greater than every temptation that trips us up. And the presence that is greater than anything that could ever try to trap us.

You and I are carrying the presence of God inside of us. Jesus broke into human history, and He brought with Him salvation, freedom, forgiveness, and hope and deposited these things in us. These are the things His presence brings to mankind. By the Holy Spirit, He placed all of this inside us so we can release His presence in every situation. When His presence is released, faith is released and miracles happen; sin is avoided and victory is assured; and hope is poured out, making even the worst situations bearable. It is the character of God released from within us. That is incarnation demonstrated.

Our incarnation can be demonstrated in many ways. Serving love by the bowlful in a downtown soup kitchen. Delivering dignity through conversation with seniors at a nursing center. Transferring faith through a handwritten note to a recent divorcée. Or perhaps releasing much needed forgiveness in a broken relationship.

There is a move back toward demonstrating the character of God in the business arena. Dr. Thomas K. Tewell leads a group of business people in a lecture series called "Faith@Work." In this series, he urges business people to become "points of distribution" for the love of God in the marketplace. Employees and bosses alike need to see the life of God lived out in everyday Christianity. The results will be a more ethical and humane workplace where the character of God can find greater appreciation and acceptance.

The incarnation of Christ must also be demonstrated in the arts. During the Renaissance much of the best art centered on biblical themes. Through the years the demonstration of incarnation by these artists has touched thousands of lives. Somehow I wonder if stuffed animals, Bible action heroes, and velvet glow-in-the-dark Jesus pictures carry the same incarnational power.

Music has come a long way in the church. However, much of the praise music we enjoy never reaches the ears of the world. I was doing a national singles conference and participated in a panel with a very popular Christian recording group. There were about three thousand students in the room with an open mic. The crowd asked the normal questions: "How long have you been married?" "What's it like to record an album?" I've never had a recording contract or been married, but I could have answered those questions. After about fifteen or twenty questions like these, I chimed in.

"I have a question," I said. The leader of the band said, "Go ahead," so I continued, "Obviously you guys are successful. Your records are played all over the country. But how do you survive in Christian music when it is the stepchild of the music industry?" Everyone in the room suddenly woke up, but nobody said a word. The band just looked at me like my dog does and wondered where their thumbs were.

That question was my passive-aggressive, veiled way of saying that most of the lyrics in Christian music are incarnational but the ministry of Christian music often is not. Christian music all too often shines the light in an already lighted room, like a church building or a Christian music festival. In order for Christian music to become incarnational, it must take its lighted message to the club circuit and to the opening acts of world-famous touring bands.

A friend of mine attends a church where the worship band plays five nights a week at a popular nightclub. Another friend of mine in Memphis plays drums in a worship band every week but plays at the casinos to make her living. Why don't Christian bands put together a sound and music that would provide a great opening act for top-name billboard artists? Who says a Christian artist has to sing only songs that tell about Jesus? Can't their songs support the godly values of light and life?

The music of the church talks about our incarnation, but it does it to a crowd that is largely already a part of God's kingdom. Music should demonstrate our incarnation plainly so the world can see. We have too many Christian bands and not enough bands of Christians.

Christian literature (and I use this term loosely) now has its own section in many bookstores entitled "Christian Fiction." Doesn't the world struggle enough with believing our story? Do we have to reinforce their thinking that we're making this stuff up? Incarnation happens in the mainstream of life as we live out our lives. Incarnation is best viewed as an integrated part of the threads weaving the tapestry of our lives. Incarnation is obscured when the only place it is observable is within Christian circles of influence.

Hunger for spiritual literature is increasing both in the private and business sectors. Incarnation literature should be high-quality fiction, prose, and self-help material written and distributed to help people see and touch the things of God for themselves.

Laurie Beth Jones is the author of three such books: *Jesus CEO*, *Jesus in Blue Jeans*, and *Jesus, Inc*. All three present biblical principles of leadership and management for the modern-day businessperson. They are found in the business section of bookstores. Anne Lamott has written *Traveling Mercies: Some Thoughts on Faith*. She has also written the novels *Bird by Bird* and *Crooked Little Heart*. Both of these women are professed believers. Their incarnational works are targeted toward and sold to people outside the confines of the traditional Christian market.

I should, however, offer my own disclaimer at this point. I am communicating these thoughts in a book that will bear the imprint of a Christian publisher. If you could, would you consider going back to the bookstore where you purchased this volume and kindly move all the copies to the self-help section…next to the bestsellers, please…in alphabetical order…jacket face out?

Hollywood spends billions of dollars each year producing movies. Multiplex theaters are cropping up all over the country. People spend millions of dollars every weekend just to be transported into a life that is not their own so they can escape the all-too-real world they live in. The message of incarnation has the real life they are longing for. Unfortunately, most Christian movies are produced and packaged in such a way that the audience who needs to see the demonstration of incarnation won't spend eight dollars to watch it.

The nature of incarnation is not to escape the culture to create our own culture but rather to go into the existing culture to release the presence of God. This requires rock-solid faith. This requires courage and character. This requires that the presence of God be fully alive in us.

The real evidence of your personal incarnation of Christ will be the first time someone comes up to you and says, "I've seen Jesus, and He is you."

2. *Reconciliation* Restores Light

> Christ has made peace between God and man: "*And on earth, peace among men with whom He is pleased.*" (Luke 2:14)

God establishes peace on the earth through the people with whom He is well pleased. His peace is established on earth one life at a time. As that life grows and becomes more like Christ, God's peace will rule a little more of the earth. But the beginning of peace is and always will be one man or one woman being made right with God.

The framework of a life without peace is separated and exposed. Separated from the life and light of God. Exposed to the full influence of darkness. Jesus, God's peace, reconnects and covers the life He cohabits. Reconnects that life with the eternal life and light of God. Covers that life from the darkness, forever breaking the consuming control the darkness once held. The Prince of Peace, Jesus, is the only possible reconciliation between God and man.

This Peacemaker came to earth and successfully lived out a perfect life—no sin, no error in thought or deed. "*He made Him who knew no sin to be sin on our behalf, so that we might become the righteousness of God in Him*" (2 Corinthians 5:21). His perfect life became the one acceptable sacrifice to bring peace between God and man. His life and death make it possible for us to live out the righteousness of God on this earth. His life was God initiated, and His death was God planned. Reconciliation is God's loving man, providing one complete, unduplicable way for peace to be established and lived out upon the earth.

Most of us never realize the power that is available to us through being reconciled to God. We only recognize the limited power we have within ourselves. For those of us who are in Christ Jesus, our identity is not in ourselves but in Him. And as such, the basis of our power is also in Him. When we recognize His position in us, we then begin to grasp our position in Him and confidently live the life of peacemakers of God on earth.

"*And on earth peace among men with whom He is pleased.*" This is our message. "There is peace!" This is our work. "This peace is available to all!" Jesus came not just for personal ministry but also to raise up a community of peacemakers. While on earth, Jesus demonstrated ultimate peace. If true peace is to be a reality on earth, every individual must receive it. But every individual must first hear that the way to peace has been provided. This is why God has given us the ministry of reconciliation: "*He has committed to us the word of reconciliation. Therefore, we are ambassadors for Christ, as though God were making an appeal through us; we beg you on behalf of Christ, be reconciled to God*" (2 Corinthians 5:19–20).

The world needs peacemakers. We are the mouthpieces of God. God's peace resides in us, and He will put us in situations where we must personally draw on His peace. As we do, we "flesh out" the peace of God in real-life situations in ways others can understand. Our ministry of reconciliation is to make peace observable. We become the living Jesus the world needs to see. For many people still in darkness, this is the dawning of light that God uses to show them their need for His peace.

We are not lawyers somehow arguing people into peace. Nor are we salesmen peddling peace for $29.95 an issue. Peace is seen through a reconciled life lived out in a chaotic world. That's a powerful enough message. When your life is validated by peace, the words that you use to communicate that peace to others are of less concern. When anyone in need of peace observes a life that is full of the light of peace, they see it, they know what it is, and they want it.

3. *Supernatural* Shows Light

> The supernatural is the normal dimension of God: "*And an angel of the Lord suddenly stood before them.... And sud-*

> *denly there appeared with the angel a multitude of the heavenly host.*" (Luke 2:9, 13)

God exists beyond our natural ability to see and comprehend. Unless acted upon by God, our finite realm limits our ability to see the supernatural. In Luke 2, the angels suddenly appeared in front of the shepherds, and the invisible barrier that separates the natural from the supernatural was split. For those few moments, the natural experienced the supernatural.

It is in this supernatural dimension that we touch God and His power. When Christ steps out of heaven and steps in to live in our lives, the barrier between the natural and supernatural is forever broken. The supernatural dimension of God's life is ever present in us. Wherever we go, whatever we do, we bring the possibility of the supernatural with us. Within us are the limitless, supernatural resources of God waiting to be released in the very real situations of our lives.

But it is these very real situations of life that pose the most intimidating barrier we must cross. Everything in life is physical, takes up space, and has an impact on something else. This circle of life seems unchangeable. We believe only the things we can see, touch, smell, and prove by some scientific test. By default, we have chosen to operate out of this fundamental principle.

We have chosen to face the situations of life from our touch-it, smell-it, and prove-it default position. The supernatural is beyond this. The supernatural has broken the unbreakable circle of life. The power of the supernatural is untouchable, odorless, and very often beyond the proof of any scientific laboratory or research. It is this unseen and unknown territory that is the place where we fight the real battles of life.

Our struggle may seem to be with the boss or the teller at the bank, but our real struggle is found in the supernatural. These situations provide the perfect opportunity for Christ to reign in our world. When the boss pushes us to the limit, this is an opportunity for Christ's power to be made visible through us. The real choice we face is greater than the words we choose to respond to the boss. The real choice is the choice to release the light of God into a dark situation.

Understanding the supernatural living in us helps us see that our world is not static but dynamic. And our role in the expansion of God's kingdom is crucial. Our dark world is in desperate need of people who understand the supernatural. The world needs to see a people free from the controlling influence of the natural world. It needs to see a people whose reality is the kingdom of God reigning through their lives and the demonstration of God's power through every situation they face.

I had lunch with the camp director of one of the many camps I do every summer. As we sat across from each other, I was thinking about how to get to town for some real food. But he wanted to talk about his son. "You know, his mother and I raised him in the church and taught him the right way to live life," he started. I could hear the pain rising in his voice. "But the past few years, he seems to have just twisted off. He's doing all the things we taught him to stay away from. Sometimes I think he's so far gone that he'll never come back."

I asked him, "How old is your son?"

"Twenty-three," he said.

I told him, "I speak to this age group all the time. They are caught up in the thinking that God is not the center of everything and that their situation dictates the best choices for solving whatever problems they face. They look for answers in places you and I would never look. But rest assured, the things you and your wife taught him will be very important to him. He may never tell you this, but those key truths will be the baseline measurement he will use to make many of his decisions. He'll be back."

This man works with thousands of teenagers every year, and even though he loves them all, his greatest concern at that moment was for his own son. He let me see his pain, not knowing what I would say or do. I was able to release His light into this man's troubled thoughts.

As containers of God's presence, we go into life to release Him into our circumstances. And as we release God into life for others to see, we truly are peacemakers and powerbrokers. If you are a believer, you, too, carry the supernatural power of God inside of you.

4. *Glorification* Generates Light

> God is acknowledged as the Supreme Ruler through our lives: "*And the glory of the Lord shone around them.... Glory to God in the highest.*" (Luke 2:9, 14)

In these two verses, the word *glory* is used in two ways. In verse 14 *glory* refers to God's position: "*Glory to God in the highest.*" In verse 9 the same word, *glory,* is shown taking action on God's behalf, actually generating light around the shepherds: "*And the glory of the Lord shone around them.*"

This was and is such good news because it announced the beginning of the destruction of the enemy's claim to the earth. Christ's life, death, burial, and resurrection defeated death, hell, and the grave and voided Satan's legal hold on the earth. The cross is the ultimate expression of the word *glory.* The victory Christ won on the cross forever destroyed the legal hold Satan had on the earth. His death makes it possible for anyone to pass from death into life, to move from darkness into light. The cross literally breaks the control Satan has on an individual life. God's glorious victory is in the cross of Christ.

Someone must enforce the victory of the cross. The victory is complete, but it must be personally received. As you and I live in this dark world, we must enforce the victory of the cross. Our lives must release the glory of God; we must represent the work of the cross in our lives. Wherever we meet darkness, we carry within us the active glory of God waiting to be released and demonstrated through us.

Here are some simple suggestions to glorify God in your world:

- *Don't blow up abortion clinics and kill those who don't agree with your politics.*

  Society wants to make abortion a political issue. It is always presented in legal terms: "Women have a right to determine what happens inside their own bodies." People want to make a legal issue out of a moral issue.

  Abortion is an issue the church must address. It is an issue that we, as people of light, need to answer. Abortion is an issue of character. Well-meaning believers have chosen to attack the issue head-on while the subtle forces of darkness have outflanked the light and won the abortion battle inside the minds of the public. The battle will not be won in the courts. It will not be won by planting bombs. The battle will be won as we release the power of God's glory into life's situations. As God's people release glory, we will step in and help women make moral decisions about their reproductive rights. Not nearly enough has been done to publish the moral message about abortion. Either we believe in the power of God's published word or we don't. If we do, let's release the glory of God into this darkness by speaking and living lives that reflect our beliefs.

- *Focus more on getting the Ten Commandments into your family's life and less on getting them on the wall of the school.*

  Do we really believe that people murder because they don't know that it is wrong? I mean, do we really believe that if we put the Ten Commandments on the wall, some kid with a gun in his hand would say, "Well look there, murder is wrong. I didn't know that. I'm going back to class." Do we really believe that?

- *Don't sleep with people who are not your spouse.*

  Just in case this isn't clear enough, let me rephrase it: Don't sleep with people who are not your spouse.

- *Give up racial hatred.*

  If you're a Christian, *you* are the minority.

- *Be friends with someone outside of your cultural background.*

  Do this not so you can win them to Christ but just so you can be friends with them.

- *Don't try to moralize to people who live in darkness.*

Trying to get people with darkened hearts to live like believers is like trying to get Jesus and Satan to sit down for a nice, quiet, relaxing dinner. It's just not going to happen.

- *Dedicate yourself to living the light of Christ.*

  If we want a better world, we will have to surrender to the call to be the light of God while we're here. The more living lights we have that are releasing the presence of God into this world, the less room there is for darkness. The more people we have who are releasing the character of God into this world, the more friendships are changed, the more families are changed, the more lives are changed, and the more society is changed and reorganized. God wants to drop people into positions in companies and retail stores and schools who are living containers of His presence, releasing what they are holding. Over time, the presence of God begins to spread, and that is glory.

This is the simplest way I can put it: What God does *to* us, He does *through* us.

It is God's presence living in us that is released as we encounter the lives of others. But what is it that provides the real power to energize God's presence to impact another life? That is the subject of our next chapter.

Take your skill or the service that you do professionally and find ways to offer it freely to those who cannot afford it. Find ways to do this so that you can remain anonymous.

FIVE

Task Light

PRAYING TO WIN

Jesus entered the world as light invading the darkness. He comes to live in believers to enable us to continue invading the darkness. The *lit* life "fleshes" out the character of Christ in the presence of darkness and confronts it authoritatively through prayer. "*The effective prayer of a righteous man can accomplish much*" (James 5:16) because his life is *lit* with the visible character of the righteousness of Christ invading the darkness wherever it is found.

The light has power, and as believers use it, the light advances with authority. We fearlessly take our stand in the strength, power, and authority of God's Word. The light becomes more than something we talk about or sing about; it becomes our identity. The light in us becomes something the darkness around us fears and flees.

Companies are constantly downsizing and laying off employees. The airwaves are flooded with car commercials trying to make us believe that we can't live without the newest model. Credit-card companies target high-school students, trying to get them hooked on living in debt even before they get out of college. The bottom line of profit drives all these things.

For some of us, the only time we pray is when we wake up in the morning and say, "Oh, God!" Down here on Planet Bottom Line, we see the facade of these kinds of business practices for what it is, and we are in desperate need of something authentically powerful.

But power seems to be in limited supply. People will look almost anywhere to find it—astrology, amulets, even a vegan lifestyle. They'll look to gurus of near-death experiences. These are people who want to tell you about the afterlife because they died and came back. Why were these people sent back? Didn't they make the cut? That's the equivalent of getting up to the doors of a famous nightclub, finding out your name is not on the list, and being sent back home. All their stories sound the same: They zoom through a long, dark tunnel toward a bright light. Hey man, that's the light from the TV you forgot to turn off before you went to bed! Why would you want to listen to someone who couldn't get in the door?

Then there is Eastern religion, which points out into more directions than a Hindu god. Eastern mysticism has reincarnated itself so many times that it's gone through more identities than Madonna.

Remember the Ouija Board? The only thing it ever pointed to was that Satan is a very slow speller. I was held back a grade for spelling that slowly, and he has an entire kingdom...what's that about?

Today the Ouija Board has been replaced by psychics and channelers who, for a small fee, will connect you to the other side by playing a Yanni CD, turning on a black light, and rubbing their hands around a crystal ball. They shuffle some cards and speak in vague generalities like, "You had a teacher in the seventh grade who was a woman." And, "Someone in your family has an uncle." They sound like they're playing the board game Guesstier: "Oh I'm getting—sounds like H—one vowel—it's personal. 'Hi!' They want me to tell you, 'Hi.' That will be two hundred dollars, please." The two things you can be confident about with psychics are (1) they are going to take your money, and (2) they know how to operate a neon sign.

Cards, crystals, and pyramids. What do these things remind you of? Vegas! That's right, Eastern religion has been reincarnated as a casino where everyone is hopping from one game to the next in hopes of copping a metaphysical buzz. All of it is controlled by the cosmic Mafia, who is playing for keeps. The house minimum is your soul, and when the game is over, no one goes home a winner.

The rise of metaphysics has made the supernatural more visible to people than ever before. It has unleashed a revival of the dark side. What many people are experiencing is real—and very dangerous.

Believers must move out of the natural and stop wasting time praying pointlessly. While praying with a group of people, I once heard a guy ask God, "Why does it feel so good when I rub my eyes really hard?" I'm sure he's still waiting for an answer.

Jesus viewed prayer as an act of war. Christ's prayer life focused on confronting darkness with the light of God in any given circumstance. Through prayer Jesus took on what had been stolen by Satan in order to restore it to its natural, God-given use.

It is interesting to note that Jesus always prayed without fear, timidity, or doubt. "Great enjoyment" is the phrase that sums up Jesus' prayer life. He possessed such confidence in the face of darkness! Jesus had fun fighting. He knew that the cosmic Mafia was on earth illegally, and He came to kick it out.

He saw every kind of hurt in places that needed light. Just getting answers to prayer wasn't His focus; rather, it was driving out darkness so the light of God could come in.

Prayer was Jesus' greatest tool for change, and it is ours as well. What does effective prayer look like? What are the principles on which this kind of prayer functions? That is the focus of this chapter.

"The effective prayer of a righteous man can accomplish much." Another way of saying this is, "The prayer life of a person of character brings about great results." That's my personal paraphrase of James 5:16. It is imperative that Christians understand prayer and its connection to character.

Alert to the Static

The power of prayer is affected by an individual's character. Anytime you are praying and you find yourself asking, "Why isn't this working?" ask yourself if there is anything in your life that could be blocking your prayers.

Most of the time it's the subtle things in our lives that make up the interference that keeps our prayers from getting through. Static generally has a cause. If we can identify the cause, we should be able to clear out the blockage to our prayers. And more often than not, the static boils down to one of three things: unconfessed compromises, unresolved conflict, or uncontrolled concerns.

1. Unconfessed Compromises

These are those things or areas in our lives where we've knowingly compromised. It could be in business or finances or relationships or personal, private habits—things we've tucked away in our hearts.

> *If I regard wickedness in my heart* [if I allow compromise in my heart], *the Lord will not hear.* (Psalm 66:18)

Compromises are done knowingly. They are done when we put ourselves ahead of God, when we tell ourselves we are going to do whatever feels right to us, no matter what the cost. It's very difficult for us to get on our knees in prayer when we are living in that kind of rebellion.

2. Unresolved Conflict

Sometimes our relationship with God seems crowded because, whether we know it or not, we carry every other human relationship into our relationship with Him. Conflicts at work, at home, with our family, in trashed romances—all of these affect the way we pray.

> *For if you forgive others for their transgressions, your heavenly Father will also forgive you.* (Matthew 6:14)

> *Let all bitterness and wrath and anger and clamor and slander be put away from you, along with all malice.... Forgiving each other, just as God in Christ also has forgiven you.* (Ephesians 4:31–32)

We have such a casual attitude toward God. We close our eyes and lay out our well-meaning prayers with emotion and sincerity, all the while thinking that the way we live our lives has no bearing on the power and effectiveness of our prayers.

If you ask to borrow my car and I agree, you would come over to my house to get it. Suppose that as you walk through the yard to the front door, my little dog begins yapping at you, and then he starts biting at your shoestrings. While he is hanging on to your shoe, you kick him across the yard—then you look up and see me watching the whole thing through the window. Don't you think it would be a little harder now for you to ask for the keys to my car? Think about it. My dog is staggering backward across the yard, and you have your hand out and a cheesy grin on your face. But that's the way we come to God. We have compromises and unresolved conflict in our lives, and we ignore them as if they weren't really there.

3. Uncontrolled Concerns

Eating is necessary, but there are eating disorders that are treatable or, in a sense, "masterable." We have to sleep, but some people have perfected the fourteen-hour sleep day. We have to wear clothes and live somewhere, but when these concerns of life master us, they become a hindrance to prayer.

> *For all that is in the world, the lust of the flesh and the lust of the eyes and the boastful pride of life, is not from the Father, but is from the world.* (1 John 2:16)

When life is disciplined, there are fewer hindrances to the life of prayer. Prayer is not an event. In a life that is self-controlled, prayer flows naturally, unhindered, and without limitations.

> *Walk by the Spirit, and you will not carry out the desire of the flesh.* (Galatians 5:16)

Jesus lived a static-free life. His life was a life of total surrender. He is the ultimate example of a mastered life. When He comes to live inside us, He creates a drive for our lives to be lived static free. In order to pray as Jesus prayed, we must make sure that any hindrances are removed. We must be alert to static.

Attack the Source

No matter where Jesus went, His life of prayer was experienced. Jesus prayed that diseases would be healed, and they were. He prayed that the dead would be raised, and they were. But the focus of His prayers was not that miracles would happen. The focus of His prayers was that darkness would be destroyed in the lives of people.

Jesus traveled from town to town, and wherever He went He targeted darkness wherever He found it. He took the battle to the source. If the focus of His visits had been to perform miracles, the impact would have been little more than that of a traveling medicine man. Miracles were the direct result of His being focused on the destruction of darkness in people's lives.

We must attack satanic forces wherever we find them. Darkness engulfs the world, and there is no lack of opportunities we have to attack the darkness. Our greatest limitation will be our own fears and desires. And our greatest fears arise out of our ignorance about how God expects us to face the darkness. The plan Jesus used to attack darkness was to pray authoritatively. In Matthew 21:18–22, Jesus gave His disciples an object lesson in praying with authority.

The cursing of the fig tree in this story is the only destructive miracle Christ performed. He and his disciples were on their way to Jerusalem. Along the road on the hills just outside Jerusalem grew some tasty fig trees. Their leaves were thick, giving the impression that sweet figs were there for the taking. Jesus took both hands and searched among the leaves for a fig, but He found that the tree was fruitless.

He cursed the fig tree and said that no one should eat fruit from it ever again. The tree withered instantly. The disciples immediately looked through their backpacks for anything that resembled a fig. Then they asked Jesus how it was that the tree withered so quickly.

Jesus used this living illustration to demonstrate to His disciples that effective prayer attacks the source of the problem.

> *And Jesus answered and said to them, "Truly I say to you, if you have faith and do not doubt, you will not only do what was done to the fig tree, but even if you say to this mountain, 'Be taken up and cast into the sea,' it will happen. And all things you ask in prayer, believing, you will receive."* (Matthew 21:21–22)

This kind of prayer battles the darkness. Jesus tells us that we are not speaking *to* God about the darkness so much as we are speaking *for* God to the darkness. We are not asking that the fig tree be cursed or the mountain be moved; we are speaking God's Word, commanding it to wither or move. This kind of prayer invades the enemy's territory and establishes the kingdom.

This is exactly what Jesus did wherever He went. In Mark 9 a man brought his son to Jesus so that He could cast out a demon that had plagued the boy since childhood. The demon often threw the boy in fire or water to kill him. The man said to Jesus, "*I told Your disciples to cast it out, and they could not do it*" (Mark 9:18). The Bible says that Jesus looked at the boy and spoke to the demon and that the demon left him. Jesus' disciples came to Him afterward and asked Him why they had been unable to cast out the demon. Jesus let them know that part of praying, believing, and receiving is speaking God's will and Word directly to the source of the situation.

In Luke 9:1–2, Jesus gave His disciples authority to speak to sickness and demons, and they would obey them. The disciples went out proclaiming the kingdom of God and performing miracles like Jesus. When we face darkness, we are confronting the principalities that are from the pit. We are not in a war of the flesh; we are in a war of the spirit against the kingdom of darkness. The *lit* life is the life of God living in us and confronting darkness on a bloody battlefield, winning strategic and decisive battles day by day.

Through effective prayer, light is taken into specific situations.

When faced with the light, darkness moves into retreat mode. This kind of prayer is something we do because of who we are in Christ. It is the natural outflow of a *lit* life.

Approach in Surrender

If you have faith… (Matthew 21:21)

If our praying is to be powerful and effective, it must be approached in surrender to God. It must be found in our surrender to His authority and will. This kind of faith is choosing to believe that when we speak God's Word directly to a situation, He will bring it to pass because it is His will and it is what He is already doing on earth.

We all have the same amount of faith. Faith isn't measurable. Answered prayer is not based on how well we develop that hard-to-find faith muscle. That would make faith a skill, and that would make the exercising of faith something other than faith. It would cease being something outside our abilities and control and become something we can develop, like great biceps or six-pack abs.

We are not producing anything on our own. We are only distributing what has already been produced in heaven. We are God's pivotal players on earth. God has chosen not to fulfill His will outside of the process of prayer. He does nothing on earth apart from prayer. The bottom line is this: God works through our prayers, by faith.

Every one of us is facing mountains in our life. Some of us are dealing with habits or relationships that are on the brink of destroying some part of our lives. Some of us are dealing with the loss of a job, the death of a dream, or both. Some of us are dealing with bad family relations. Some of these things have been in our lives for a long time, and they qualify as mountains.

Perhaps you look at your mountain and think that there is no way it is ever going to get any better. You think there is no way you will ever get free of the burden or the pain. You are intimidated and think your mountain is immovable. It's easy to talk yourself out of praying or to pray half-heartedly and hope God takes care of it.

When Jesus turned to His disciples and said, "If you have faith," He was telling them not to look at the size of the mountain or the size of their faith but to look at the strength of God. Surrender says, "God, I am surrendered to who You are and what You want to do in this situation. I recognize that as Your child, I have Your authority and power in this earth, and I have the right to pray into this situation. I speak to this situation in Your name."

Anchored in Scripture

...and do not doubt. (Matthew 21:21)

How can anyone pray while doubting? Prayer and doubt don't mix any more than opera singers and balsa wood furniture.

> *But he must ask in faith without any doubting, for the one who doubts is like the surf of the sea, driven and tossed by the wind. For that man ought not to expect that he will receive anything from the Lord.* (James 1:6–7)

Anchoring prayer to Scripture keeps us from floating into the danger zones of selfishness, pride, arrogance, and control. Praying out of the authority of Scripture keeps us from making a spectacle out of the results of prayer. The world is more impressed with effective prayers that actually change things than it is with empty prayers that result in things remaining the same. The world is crying out for change, not a chance for change. The Scripture gives us discernment in how to pray and attack the source of evil. It gives us guidance on how to pray so that the world can see things change.

The will of God and the Word of God never contradict. The way to pray without doubting is to pray in line with the will and the Word of God. Praying the Word of God is like having the final go ahead before we ever ask anything. It's God's giving us permission to ask for what He has already prepared to give us. Knowing what the Word says about our situation increases our faith. Before praying, immerse yourself in Scripture; fill yourself with the Word. Then pray it back. You'll do it without doubting.

Chapter Five

I was speaking at a summer camp and drove into town late one night to get a snack. About the only place open was McDonald's, so I hit the drive-through. When it was my turn, I rolled down the window and gave my order: "Yes, I'll have a large yogurt twist in a cup and some McDonaldland cookies." The lady repeated my order over a speaker system that had more static than a dryer full of double knit bowling shirts. Why would a business spend fifty-eight thousand dollars on a sound system that gives the customer the impression they care even less than they do?

I drove up to the window and handed the lady my money. She handed me a box of cookies and a small water cup of yogurt. I handed the cup of yogurt back to her and reminded her that I had ordered the large cup, not the "shooter" size. She took the cup back inside, and I waited. While she was gone, the clothes I was wearing went out of style and came back in.

She came back carrying the forty-two-ounce, super-duper-size drink cup filled with yogurt. In one motion, she hoisted the cup with both hands and kicked open the drive-through window. The window flew open, and she nearly dropped three pounds of yogurt in my lap. I regained my composure and asked if the large size comes with a free pair of Depends. "If I drink all of this," I said, "I'll need them."

She started to close the window, but I stopped her. "Seriously, ma'am, do I get a spoon with the yogurt?"

She looked at me like my dog does when I practice my jokes on him. "A spoon?" she said.

I paused and said, "Yeah, you know, it's white, has a handle, and is concave on one end." Her expression never changed; she just closed the window and was gone long enough for me to change my oil and rotate my tires.

Yogurt melting, cookies half-eaten, the window opened again. She held out a plastic spoon in an environmentally safe plastic wrapper and asked me, "Is this it?" I grabbed the spoon out of her hand and said through clenched teeth, "Wait right there. I'll try it out and let you know."

The point is, when we pray, we can't be presumptuous. God is not a drive-through window. We can't expect to roll up to God arrogantly assuming that He will answer our prayer exactly as we want it. If we want our prayers to be powerful and effective, we have to pray and speak the will and Word of God.

Here are some unanswerable prayer requests:

- "God, let me pass the test because I didn't study. Please let me sit by somebody smart." Or, "Please give me a limber neck and really good vision."

- "God, please change that person; he's really a jerk." We pray that prayer because we don't want God to change us. We don't mind confronting God about another person, but we don't want God confronting us about our own shortcomings.

- The great prayer of celebrity wannabes: "God, make me famous so I can humbly serve You." Hello. Let me be famous and popular so I can be Your servant?

- If you're praying that your team will win the game…forget it. God doesn't even like sports.

- If you're praying for your favorite soap stars to get out of their most recent affairs or at least avoid getting caught, mark it down: God won't answer that one.

The motive of these kinds of prayers is selfishness, not the Word and will of God. Whatever your need is, find out what the Scripture has to say about it and then pray in line with that. You'll find power and effectiveness, and I promise you'll like the answers you get.

The focus of our praying is not to have our own needs met. We are praying the will of God and the rule of God into our circumstances. When we pray the Word and will of God, we are releasing the will of the living God into those circumstances. We bring the freedom of Christ to bear, and we destroy the grip that darkness holds.

When we pray the will and Word of God, we are taking the light of

His Word into places that are covered in darkness. If we do not pray, the darkness continues to rule in those places. When we pray selfishly, the darkness increases.

We are called to live, walk, and pray as children of light. We are given the tremendous responsibility to pray the light of Christ into every situation we encounter. We do this as we pray the will and Word of God. To pray the Word is to pray to win.

Ask Specifically

But even if you say… (Matthew 21:21)

I have no sense of direction, and I have to travel all the time. If someone says, "Just go north," I'm thinking, *Is that left or right?* I really don't know. I speak in little towns all the time, and just having to get to my destinations has helped me learn new ways of trusting God, especially when I don't have a map and I have to make one of my best dyslexic guesses.

I was in North Carolina looking for a church where I was scheduled to speak. I went into an old-fashioned drugstore to get directions. I know it was an old-fashioned drugstore because it had a real soda fountain. I asked the guy working there how to get to the church. I told him it had some unbelievable name like Harmony, Unity, or Friendship. (Ain't it fun to pretend?)

This guy said, "Well, yeah, I'll tell you what to do." He made a broad, sweeping motion with his entire arm and pointed off in some nondescript direction. "You just take this road and head straight out of town until you see a broken stick."

I clarified, "A broken stick?"

He nodded. "Yeah, it's hanging over the barbed wire on the corner, and then you make a left and keep goin' until you see a broken chair. Then turn right. That road will take you there."

I'm thinking, *So I look for a stick on a wire and a broken chair.* (And you thought Harmony Baptist Church was funny.) I'm not making this stuff up.

The trouble with people giving directions is that very often what they give is completely missing what you asked for...directions. When I go to the mall and ask where the men's department is, I get, "It's over that way." That's helpful. Is it more over and less that way, or less over and more that way? I mean, I've got money to spend. Can't you at least give me specific directions to the cashier?

But this is how we pray. We talk to God in directionless language. "Well, God, if that is what You want, that would be a good idea, and it will make me happy. But if it's not Your will, then, uh...you know, God...work it out, uh...you know. Amen." It's no wonder there's no power in our prayers.

Remember the fig tree that Jesus cursed? Mark is careful to point out that "*it was not the season for figs*" (Mark 11:13). Because of where that fig tree was located, it should have had fruit earlier than most others. But for whatever reason, the tree had no fruit.

Man was not the only thing affected at the fall. The cosmic Mafia's fall to earth affected the earth itself. The Mafia unleashed havoc on creation. Jesus saw the fruitless fig tree as an object of the fall, so when He spoke against it, He was in fact cursing the curse that creation was under.

In effect He was saying, "I have come to bring light to this darkened world. My light is the light to mankind and creation." He addressed the darkness where He found it. He didn't avoid it and hope that it would go away. He confronted and cursed the darkness—and it withered.

The fig tree immediately withered, and that impressed the disciples. What ought to impress us is that Jesus knew that the purpose of prayer was to undo the work of the enemy. Prayer brings about the present rule of the kingdom of God on the earth. The tree withered in the same way that the power of the enemy will wither at its root forever. Jesus spoke the curse on the tree not because it was fruitless but because He saw it as part of creation under the curse of darkness.

Our call to use the weapon of prayer is aimed specifically at uprooting and cursing darkness wherever we find it. The focus of prayer is not on the miraculous but on instilling light and dispelling darkness. Specific needs take on new meaning when they are considered in the bigger picture of releasing light into the darkness of every situation. It's not that we shouldn't ask for healing and address specific needs in prayer, but we must address them in the context of bringing the rule of the kingdom of God into every situation.

For just a moment, consider a tree living in creation just as God intended it. Revelation 22:2–3 describes such a tree: "*On either side of the river was the tree of life, bearing twelve kinds of fruit, yielding its fruit every month.... There will no longer be any curse.*" There is no "off season" for fruit bearing. The tree constantly has fruit because there is no curse.

Now take the man who lives the character of Christ. This is man living in the light as God intended. Psalm 1:3 says, "*He will be like a tree firmly planted by streams of water, which yields its fruit in its season and its leaf does not wither; and in whatever he does, he prospers.*" This man bears fruit and does not wither. Whatever he does prospers. This is the picture of living in the light. This is mankind and the world as God intended them to be. This is what we are to pray for...specifically.

Anticipate the Solution

...it will happen. (Matthew 21:21)

We've been conditioned to think that the only type of effective prayer is the type that is answered instantly. But answered prayer is not necessarily immediately recognized. That's not to say God's answer isn't immediate. It is to say that it can take some time for us to recognize the solution God gives.

We live in an instant society. There is a principle called gigabirritation (pronounced gig-a-bir-i-ta-tion). It simply means that the faster our computers are, the quicker we get irritated at how long we have to wait for the graphics to download. Broadband Internet will soon give way to gigabit connectivity that will be so fast we'll all be able to answer our e-mail before we get it. We have Minute Rice that is done in thirty seconds. Microwave brownies. Single-serve wieners. Now we even have elastic plastic wrap that looks like little-bitty, colored hair nets to put over our leftover containers.

Effective prayer may not be answered in an instant, and most likely it won't be. But Jesus is telling us that if we have faith and don't doubt, it will happen. It's one thing to ask in faith; it is another to keep on believing in faith. This kind of faith is based not in our ability to maintain happy thoughts; it's based on the fact that we asked after we found out what the Scripture had to say and we prayed it back to God. If we know we have prayed God's will and Word, it will be a lot easier to keep on believing.

Pray with expectancy. Anticipate the solution. You don't know when, and you don't know how. You just know it's going to happen. Learn to rely on God and to stay faithful as He carries out His will in your situation. You can anticipate the solution He will bring because you have a confident trust in the character of God.

A key to effective prayer is that we pray it, live it, and then pray it again. I've talked with people who take their prayers and send them up in what I call "prayer flares." (You provide your own sound effects.) It's up, up, up, and away. I sure hope God sees it. Then they forget about it. They go on with their lives and never think about it again. You have to pray over your habit more than once. You have to pray over that relationship. Believe me, if something is wrong, you've had more to do with it than one prayer will cover.

If you've surrendered to the will and authority of God, if you've anchored your prayer firmly in the Word of God, and if you've asked specifically, then you have no reason not to anticipate a solution. Keep praying, keep believing, and keep waiting.

Aggressively Stand

...believing, you will receive. (Matthew 21:22)

Panama City, Florida, has some of the prettiest white-sand beaches you'll ever want to see. But there are two things I hate about the beach. One is the water; the other is that it's outside. If they could somehow move the beaches to the malls, then I'd work on my tan.

I was leaving Panama City not long ago after a hurricane had blown through the area. The traffic wasn't too bad, so I had a chance to look at the clouds. A hurricane brings in some ominous clouds. It wasn't raining hard, but it was still pretty dark for eight o'clock in the morning. The clouds were too dark and thick to let the sun through. They were moving fairly fast, but there always seemed to be more just behind them. Then something changed. There in the middle of the clouds was a hole. Through that hole I could see clear blue sky. I thought, *That's exactly what we are doing in this world.*

The light of life comes into this dark world through the character of Christ living in us. As we pray His Word, His will is released into specific situations and His authority is released, causing the darkness to retreat. Like the clouds over Panama City, we literally punch holes in the darkness, allowing the light to shine through. Prayer was the foundation of Jesus' aggressive stand against the darkness. It's where we begin too.

Find someone who is experiencing a battle with darkness and pray the Word and the will of God directly into that person's life. Don't just pray privately; go to the person personally and pray over him or her.

SIX

Fake Light

STOP GENERATING YOUR OWN LIGHT

Saul, before his name was changed to Paul, was really in the dark about what having a relationship with God is all about. To this "Hebrew of Hebrews," it meant following a huge religious rule book. Unfortunately, there are still a lot of Sauls in the church today. In case you're not sure if you're one of them, here is a list of the top ten signs that you might be religious.

You might be religious if:

10. You know all twenty-seven verses of "Just As I Am."
9. You've ever joined a Sunday-school class so you could play softball.
8. You've ever missed church with the excuse, "Hey, the disciples were fishermen."
7. You think that premarital sex is wrong because it leads to dancing.
6. You've ever prayed so loud in a restaurant that the other diners bowed their heads with you.
5. You've ever asked for a church discount at a garage sale.

4. You've ever avoided the use of cooking wine because it might make your brother stumble.

3. You've ever bummed a cigarette off a deacon.

2. You think Little-League sports are a plot to keep kids from being in church every single day.

And the number one sign that you might be religious…

1. You have a bumper sticker on your car that reads, "In case of rapture, car will swerve as my mother-in-law takes the wheel."[1]

The story of Saul who became the apostle Paul helps us see that character is more than morality. It's not just behaving in a different way or changing how we act—that's simply being well disciplined. Character is much more. Character literally is the life of Christ living in us.

Paul saw the light on his way to Damascus. All his life he had tried to have a relationship with God through the discipline of following religious "rules." What Paul discovered is that religion kills relationship. He also learned that in the pursuit of genuine character, religion is a dead end.

Everyone admired Paul for his religious achievements. Many today mistake being moral or being a "good ol' boy" for being a Christian.

Many people have grown up in church their whole lives. They have been religious but have never experienced genuine character. They've lived in homes surrounded by stacks of Bibles. Their parents have served on leadership committees. Their church pews and stained-glass windows have been dedicated in the names of dead family members. (I spoke in a church recently that actually had dedication plaques over the toilets in the bathroom—write your own joke here!) But unread Bibles and brass plaques are not going to make anyone more like Christ.

Religion is to genuine character what masks are to Halloween. (If you're religious, I mean "Harvest Festival.") None of us want to be ourselves on Halloween. That's why we buy masks and put on makeup.

And it doesn't matter how much we pay for our masks, the elastic strings always break, and we have to stop and tie them back on. Then they're too tight and hurt our heads. The legs of the costumes are always too short, and they never last through more than one fall on the concrete. Halloween costumes make us think we look like someone we're not; they make us think we look better than we do. Religion works the same way. At best religion makes us think we look better than we actually do. It's time for Christians to stop using their practice of religion as their make-believe world. Religion is counterfeit character.

In Romans 8 Paul talks about religion by using two terms: the word *law* and the word *flesh*. The word *law* at that time referred to the Old Testament. It was the Law that said, "You've got to keep all of the rules or else. You've got to keep them all or die." Be perfect or die...that's a lot like my dating life. Keeping all the rules is impossible, but that's exactly what religion encourages us to do. Let's look at four signs of someone who has chosen religion rather than character.

Focused on Scoring

> *For those who are according to the flesh* [those who are heading down the path of religion] *set their minds on the things of the flesh*. (Romans 8:5)

Religion is man's attempt to reach God. Religion believes that the only way to reach God is through performance. The only problem is, God is perfect, and to reach Him through performance requires a perfect performance. That makes religion like gymnastics; everything is scored by hundredths of points, and one slip, one misaligned landing, can cost you everything.

At the time the book of Romans was written, the Law consisted of 613 commands, 248 mandates, and 365 sacraments. If you're good at math, you've already figured out that adds up to 1,226 things that you had to do. Now, that is a lot to remember, much less keep. If you faithfully kept 1,225 and blew it on number 1,226, game over! You lose!

The mentality of performance and perfection has leaked its way into the church. Every denomination has its own set of scoring methods. For some, you have to be totally wet; for others, you have to be partially wet; for others, you have to pray to the statue; for others, you have to light a candle to get someone out of heaven's waiting room. For some, everyone has to have the same set of experiences; for others, you have to ride a bike for a year and witness to people. For still others, you have to trade in your body parts to get to ride with the Silver Surfer. Religion is unflinching and unforgiving. It doesn't take into account personal limitations. You're either in or you're out.

This scoring mind-set has been reinforced by parents and heavy-handed preachers who warn us, "There are rules, and you had better obey them." If we don't, we're told, "God's going to get you." Life becomes a matter of keeping rules and checking boxes and evaluating everything in hundredths of points. A religious person speaks of spiritual maturity in these terms: "Look how long it has been since I did that." And, "Look how faithful I've been to the church." And, "Look how good and wonderful people say I am." The religious person's life is driven by making the grade, doing well, and believing that God will be disappointed if it's not done perfectly.

I once had a very religious guy tell me, "When you stand up there and speak, you have to give people a standard to live by." That sounds really religious, but setting the standard of life is not my job. To enforce standards on people apart from them having a full and meaningful relationship with Christ is nothing more than prioritizing foolishness. My job is to introduce people to the full, complete potential of their lives lived out in the character of Christ.

The problem with a life focused on scoring is that while everyone believes there is a standard, nobody agrees on the same standard. What happens if you get to the end of your life and your scoring system is all wrong? What if you have been faithful to the wrong things? If you choose to live by performance, you have already chosen to die by performance. If you live by performance, your only chance of getting into heaven is to die on the same day as O. J. Simpson and Bill Clinton and hope God grades on a curve.

Religion is first focused on scoring. Paul reveals the second sign of a religious person in the next verse.

Fueled by Self-Effort

For the mind set on the flesh is death. (Romans 8:6)

To Paul, the objective of religion is, "I'll earn my way in. I'll do enough good things, and God will love me." Paul emphatically states that the end result of this kind of thinking is death. That sounds pretty final, doesn't it? Death is one of those things you don't come back from too often. But "trying our best" is a mind-set that fits well into the structure of our society. It is fueled by the foolish belief that we can earn our way into heaven by keeping all the laws, mandates, and commandments. If we can do that, we think, shouldn't God love us and let us in?

A religious person is someone whose entire life is fueled by self-effort. Here are some sound bites of things people say that sound spiritual but really are religious:

"I'm not perfect, but at least I'm not as bad as all the others."

Question: Who made you the judge to decide that you are not as bad as someone else? Answer: You did. Religious people fueled by self-effort decide for themselves what the standards are and how high the bar is. They decide for themselves who makes the cut. They measure themselves based on other people's behavior. This way of living has more to do with self-discipline than spiritual maturity.

"I have got to catch up on my quiet time." "If I miss my time with God, my whole day is ruined." "If your quiet time isn't in the morning, you're a wimp."

Time *with* God? When is a believer not with God? There isn't a moment when you are out of the presence of God, but religion turns devotion into a duty. Life in the Spirit is not based on a few moments in the morning. If you miss those moments, your whole day is not off.

That is just superstition. You might as well carry a rabbit's foot with you. This is not to say that setting time apart from other distractions to read and listen to God has no value. On the contrary, it's an important part of your ongoing relationship with God. Just don't make the error of mistaking your quiet time for a ritual...it's a relationship. We'll get into this more in chapter 9.

"I have to stay radical for God."

You don't keep yourself radical. Christianity is not something you empower yourself to do. You stay in the presence of God, and God empowers you to live the life.

I was walking the mall the other day and ran into someone I knew from one of the places where I speak each week. She was talking with a friend and introduced me as "the speaker guy." As soon as we met, her friend turned and walked away without saying good-bye. I asked my friend, "What's wrong with her?" She told me that the woman had been raised to believe that you are either hot or cold for Jesus, and if you're lukewarm, He will spit you out of His mouth. She had walked away because she was at a "lukewarm point" in her life. She believed that as long as she was "lukewarm," she needed to stay away from the church and those who speak for the Lord because she thought that was more honest.

This sounds very spiritual, and it preaches very well. "You are either hot or cold. You've got to be on one side or the other. If you're lukewarm, you are puke in God's mouth." But when you look at the spiritual journey of life, you see that's simply not true. All of us have mountains and valleys we go through. And don't forget the seemingly infinite middle ground where we don't seem to be frozen or on fire; we're just rocking along for God.

Religion has a subtle side. It twists Scripture. The Scriptures are given to free man from the power of controlling sin. But religion interprets Scripture in ways that lead people into another type of bondage: the bondage of self-effort.

There are incremental stages in our growth in God. People are at different stages in their growth. Some are on the warm end; some are on the cold end. And some of those on the cold end are moving toward God. God doesn't ignore people just because they aren't where He wants them to be. That's religion talking. He accepts them where they are and loves them regardless. He knows that's the only way they will ever desire to be where He wants them to be.

If there ever was a group of people that disproved our need to stay radical for God, it was the disciples, who spent over three years living with Jesus. Peter denied Him, Judas betrayed Him, and Thomas doubted Him. Yet it was this small band of men that God used to firmly establish His kingdom in this dark world.

"I come to church to worship God. I come to make it happen."

Religion makes worship a Sunday ceremony. In reality, worship is our response to God's presence. And since God is everywhere present at all times, all of life is about worship. There is not some moment when we slip into worship any more than there are moments when we slip out of worship. Religion wants us to think that we come to worship and we make worship happen. Do you see how subtle that is?

We call the big room where everyone comes together to sing and pray the "worship center." We call that one hour on Sunday morning "worship." We call the person who leads our music the "worship leader." Our tradition has taught us to limit worship to a place and, in some cases, to a leader. The Scriptures teach us that genuine worship takes place every moment of every day as we respond to God's presence in our lives.

"I am very involved in church."

But why? Many people go to church and don't know why. They've just been told they should go to church on Sundays. They show up because they had a sense that they ought to. Their going to church is not connected to anything else in life. For that matter, their church attendance is not attached to anything they do while they are there. They just go.

Religion has converted people into going to church just for the sake of going to church. They get up on Sunday and put on different clothes from the rest of the week to impress people they don't really know, much less want to know. They sit in a big room on pews that are reminiscent of the Inquisition. They sing music that sounds nothing like what they hear the rest of the week. They search for new ways to stay awake during the sermon and then feel obligated to give money...all because they *ought* to?

Church is connected to our relationship with God. Our identity in Christ is connected to who we are in His body. His body is found in the local church. The local church is where individual lights come together to celebrate and participate in the work of God's kingdom.

"Sundays are sacred."

As opposed to what other day? For a believer all days are sacred, but religion sets up Sundays to be a burdensome ritual. If you've grown up in a religious home, you know Sunday mornings are a preview of Armageddon. Your mom yells at your dad; your dad is asleep in the chair; you have one shoe with a sock and one shoe with no sock. Everyone is fighting with each other.

In the car you poke your sister in the eye. "Stop poking me!"

Your dad yells, "Listen, we're going to church, and if you don't stop it, you're going to meet Jesus before we get there. When your Sunday school teacher asks what happened, I'll deny we ever had kids. They don't know me that well; they'll believe me. Don't make me pull this car over!" Your mother reaches over the seat and puts a death grip on your shoulder.

But as soon as you step through the doors of the church, everything changes. "Hello, pastor. It's so nice to see you. How are you? Yes, the children? Lovely. My wife and I were just telling each other that on the way to church this morning."

We turn it on and off—that is religion fueled by self-effort. There's nothing sacred about it.

The truth is, Sunday morning is no more sacred than Thursday at noon or Monday evening. For believers, every day is sacred. Every day holds the opportunity for us to experience the character of Christ in every situation. Imagine this: If you experienced the character of Christ throughout your week, how much easier would Sunday mornings be?

"Yes, I have prayed the prayer."

Can there be any more anti-Christ statement than that? Listen to what you're saying: "*I* have prayed the prayer. *I* let Jesus into my life." God created the universe, and you're doing Him a favor by letting Him come and live in you? God doesn't *need* to come and live in you. He *wants* to come and live in you. He wants to put the full light of His eternal presence into your life.

"I've got a lot of stuff I need to work through."

Isn't this just another way of saying that you're going to depend on yourself to work through the things you need to? Where is God in that? Go ahead and try to fix yourself. You can do it for a while, you can change a few things, but sooner or later you'll find out that you can never really change apart from the character transformation of God's life living in you.

Working things out for yourself, fixing your own problems, is independence. God does not inhabit a life of independence. He does, however, inhabit the life that is dependent upon Him. When you've tried long enough to fix your independent self, let dependence have its day.

When spirituality is fueled by self-effort, it results in "fake light." All the statements we've listed sound very spiritual, but they aren't. They are religious. Religion is our attempt to imitate the light of God in our lives through self-effort.

There's a third sign of a religious person, as Paul shows us in the next verse.

Fatal Success

> *The mind set on the flesh is hostile…for it does not subject itself to the law of God, for it is not even able to do so.* (Romans 8:7)

Religion brings results, but they are results ending in death. They are fatal results. In this verse, Paul tells us that the flesh is hostile toward God. Anything set against God will lose. Don't even try to read it any other way. Religion has set itself against God. It is hostile to the law of God and not capable of keeping the law. Its results will inevitably be fatal.

Here are the four fatal successes of religion:

1. Mean Spirit

What religion does to people is affect their personalities. You can see it in the way they behave. You can spot religious people because they are really, really judgmental and critical, and they are cruel. They are the people who make you feel uncomfortable because you never feel quite as holy as they are. You never feel as if you measure up to their standards. I get this feeling from religious people all the time.

Religious people will not let God deal with an individual. They have to step in and play the role of the Holy Spirit and say things like, "You know, what you are doing is wrong." "You know that's a sin against God, right?" "Hey, you know you are going to hell, don't you?" They can't just leave well enough alone. They can't let God deal with people individually.

These people make you feel judged. They defend their actions by saying, "I am only doing what is biblical." Since when is being mean-spirited biblical? "Hey, I'm just doing what is right"—but they're doing it at the expense of the Spirit of God. "Hey, it's my job. I am here to convince people." They might end up convincing someone that they are right, but then nobody can stand them. The end result: They have no influence with anybody. They drive everyone away from them, including God. That is fatal success.

2. Marginal Spiritual Progress

"Mother May I"—I hated that game as a kid. I never won because the leader of the game would always give me backward steps. The person would call my name and tell me to take two baby steps backward. I would have to say, "Mother may I?" and the leader would say, "Yes you may." Then I would have to take the steps. I played the game, but I never won.

That's what happens to Christians who try to live the Christian life through religion. You can keep the rules for a while, but there's always that one rule you forget. Others can keep it, but you can't. It's like you forget to say, "Mother may I," and you have to go all the way back to the starting line.

After a while I learned that I didn't have to play the game. I could just sit by myself and say nothing. Sometimes that was more fun. At least I could win an argument with myself.

Christians who try to live life through religion will make some marginal spiritual progress, but that progress comes on the steps of self-effort and will be short lived. Almost without exception, these people end up living in a huge silence between them and God. They believe that to step back into relationship with God means they have to step back into the game they have grown to hate.

3. Many Secrets

Religion sets everyone up for failure. We know we're supposed to be the light the world can see. Since we have to "keep the light burning," we think we have to increase our level of self-effort. This includes hiding our failures.

We can't let anyone else know that we've blown it. After all, we don't know if they have blown it themselves—and being that vulnerable would be too uncomfortable for us. So we hide our sins. We disguise our weaknesses. We bury our failures. We begin to talk and walk like all the other people who are hiding their many secrets too.

4. Major Scars

Deep wounds produce major scars. Religion leads everyone to failure. The hurt of failure first shows up when we let ourselves down. We try to live up to some personal, external expectation, only to come up short. We hide that failure from everyone, including ourselves. But then we find ourselves in an even greater failure—we fail in such a way that we believe God is embarrassed. We try to hide this one from others, ourselves, and God. Ultimately we fail in a public way that we cannot hide from anyone.

The composite of these failures produces the deep wounds that leave major scars. These scars show up in many ways. Many people live with an overwhelming sense of guilt from feeling they've let God down one too many times. Some who are disciplined enough have been able to keep the standards and do the rituals, and it has produced spiritual arrogance. They have put their faith in the fact that they are very moral and can keep the law and that everyone else is on a fast track to hell. The truth is, "*There is none righteous, not even one*" (Romans 3:10). Others are guarded, never really able to be totally honest or authentic with God because they've been unable to maintain all the rules.

The problem with religion is that it manufactures a fake light. Religion is hard to recover from. And often before we recover, we use a variety of immediate fixes to try to repair our religious failures in ways that make the fake light look more real.

Fixated on Surface Solutions

> *And those who are in the flesh cannot please God.* (Romans 8:8)

In other words when we try to fix our failures—the things that are wrong with our lives—through our self-effort, in our self-motivated way, it doesn't work. Being fixated on surface solutions is behavior oriented. When we are fixated on surface solutions, the natural answer to our problem is, "I'd better go back to church," and we try one of three things: We *rededicate* our lives, we *recommit* our effort, or we *refine* our behavior.

One night while I was speaking at my weekly Bible study, one of the women who attends regularly handed me a two-page testimony that she entitled "Religious Person in Recovery." In this written testimony she told how she had lived from adolescence through early adulthood trapped in a self-imposed prison. She could not find an escape because she didn't even know she was trapped. She tried many things while looking for the freedom her heart cried out for, but nothing worked until God's Word penetrated her heart and showed her that her prison was religion.

This woman had trusted Christ as her Savior when she was a teenager. She quickly fell into the trap of thinking that the path to Christian maturity was to live a good and faithful life. She heard preachers and Sunday school teachers talk about becoming more Christlike. She understood spiritual maturity to be something she had to do, so she learned all the "rules." It only seemed natural to her that if she kept all the commandments, Jesus would love her more. She loved Him and wanted Him to love her completely. She had her quiet times, went to church at every opportunity, and always did her best to be upbeat and on fire for Jesus. On the surface these things seemed to work. Whenever she felt herself starting to slip, she went to a worship service and rededicated her life. The problem was that she found herself slipping more and more often, and her slips seemed to get worse every time. She kept her struggles and frustration a secret. She carried on as usual, and no one suspected that she was making zero headway in spiritual growth.

Ask yourself: After all the times you have walked down an aisle to make things different with God—you've wept tears of sorrow, you've written it down, you've nailed it to a cross, you've set it on fire, you've torn it up—why aren't things different? The answer is that all of these things are surface. Change does not come because you change your behavior. Change does not happen because you decide you are going to recommit. That's religion. Rededication and recommitment are just refining your behavior.

We all say things like, "I am going to do this for God.... I am going to clean up my life.... I am going to quit this.... I am going to cut that stuff out.... I am going to be a better person.... I am going to try harder." The problem is that this fixation we have with surface solutions is like putting a Band-Aid on something that is too deep to touch.

So what's the solution? Where do we find the freedom to live in the light? Where does the freedom come from?

Freeing Spirit

> *Therefore there is now no condemnation for those who are in Christ Jesus. For the law of the Spirit of life in Christ Jesus has set you free.* (Romans 8:1–2)

Free from what? Free from trying? Free from self-effort? Free from surface solutions? Yes, and also *"free from the law of sin and of death."* Free from the cycle of praying and recommitting and crying and rededicating. Free from the cycle of sin and dead-end efforts to fix problems the Law could not solve.

> *For what the Law could not do, weak as it was through the flesh, God did: sending His own Son in the likeness of sinful flesh and as an offering for sin, He condemned sin in the flesh, so that the requirement of the Law might be fulfilled in us.* (Romans 8:3–4)

Everything you and I tried to do by ourselves, Christ did, that the Law might be fulfilled in us. The Law requires that we be perfect and do everything just right. Since we can't possibly live up to that standard, God said that His Son would.

The reason there is no condemnation for those who are in Christ is that Christ removed it! He stepped into this world and took on all the sin, all the scars, all the struggles, and all the stains in our lives. He took on all our best effort, all our religious activity, all that stuff, and took it to the cross and died in our place. He did what you and I could never do for ourselves.

When we open our lives to Him, the life and light of Christ steps out of heaven and steps into our lives. Let me tell you literally what that means. When you give your life to Christ, you are uncondemnable. You cannot be condemned by sin, by law, or by religion. When you give your life to Christ, you are given His record of perfection. Upon salvation you are made perfect. Your fake light is taken away and replaced with authentic light.

God declares you to be consistent. He declares you to be pure. He gives you Jesus' performance record. You're in with God because of Christ. You don't have to work your way in; you don't have to earn your way in.

To develop the character of Christ and become light in the world, we must lose our religion. Religion is a dead end to character. Jesus wasn't religious. The only time He ever had fights was when He went to church. Think about that. The disciples certainly were not religious; they were blue-collar guys, and they worked with their hands. John the Baptist was in no way religious; he made the WWF look like the Teletubbies.

In order for Paul to become a follower of Jesus, he had to lose his rigid, self-righteous religion. He was the most religious man of his day and age, and he had to give it all up in order to follow Christ.

Here's the one step to developing true character: *Quit trying*. That's it. Just quit trying to generate your own light. Imagine what would happen if you and I were rightly related to Jesus Christ. If we stepped out of religion and into relationship, imagine the progress we would make.

I know all about this because I'm a religious person in recovery too. I was raised in the church. I grew up being told to be moral and to keep myself in line. I even went to a Christian high school. There are a lot of questionable things that I have never done in my life, and on the surface that seems pretty impressive.

I stayed away from those things out of fear, but in the kingdom that doesn't count. That is religion. I did it for the wrong reasons. What started to break me out of this religious cycle was the realization of how dim my light was and how uncaring I was toward others. I wasn't persecuting people like Saul was, but I did have a lot of arrogance. Because I was living by the rules, I thought, *Hey, why can't everyone else do it? I don't see the problem.* That's why I was horrible as a singles' counselor on a church staff. People would come to me with their spiritual struggles, and I'd say, "Well, you have just got to snap out of it."

God started to put me around people who were broken. Religion only works on people who refuse to admit they're broken. Religion doesn't work on broken people.

It's one thing to take a stand against alcohol and say, "You shouldn't drink, it's wrong." It's another thing to see what alcohol does to somebody, to see the grip it has on a person. All of a sudden you start to realize that praying a little rededication prayer does not make a marriage come back together. Signing a little card does not suddenly snap alcoholism off someone.

That's religion; that's all about the surface. Religion is a dead end to character. You will not find real character by keeping the rules. You will not find it through self-motivation or surface solutions.

What has to happen?

Do you know those little plastic communion cups? They are just about two inches tall, and they're made to hold less than an ounce of grape juice. Those little cups taught me something that I want to share with you.

I have made hundreds of decisions for God in my life—rededications, recommitments, and refinements of my behavior. I truly gave it my best shot over and over. I wanted to be different for God. I wanted my life to count.

Every time I tried my best, I failed. And every time I failed, I feared that God would take it all away from me—my ministry, my speaking, everything. I lived in that fear. I waited in that fear for His wrath to come, but it never did.

What did come was a new awakening to what God wanted. And it involved those little plastic communion cups.

God showed me that the hundreds of decisions I made for Him in my self-effort did not even begin to fill one of those little plastic cups.

My best efforts were completely insignificant in God's eyes.

What was significant was what Jesus did on that last night with His disciples, just before He was crucified. That night Jesus took a cup much larger than the plastic communion cup. He held it up and told His disciples that the cup contained Him, His blood. It didn't contain Jesus and His teaching, Jesus and His miracles, Jesus and His prayers. It just contained Jesus. A few hours after that last meal, Jesus was broken and spilled out for the sins of the world.

What God showed me was that I had tried to put myself and everything I had done into that cup and have Him call it good. All the things we have done that some may call good, all the donations we have given, all the time we have volunteered—all of this is a substitute for the real life Christ is waiting to release through us. All God wants in our little cup is nothing. Christ filled the cup of life with Himself, and He is waiting for us to drink from that real cup of life.

When I gave this talk to a group in Memphis, I gave everyone one of those plastic cups and told them that anything they put into their cup was a substitute for the blood of Christ. A guy who was there that night e-mailed me a day or so later and told me that he had put the plastic cup in his coat pocket. When he got in his car to go home, he fastened his seat belt and heard the cup crack. He had planned on filling the cup every morning with water and emptying it out as a reminder that he needed to pour everything out and come to God empty-handed. When he pulled the cup out of his pocket, he saw that it was cracked in several places. Now no matter how much water he put in, it would never hold anything. At that moment he realized exactly what God wanted from him. He knew then that all God wanted from him was for him to be open, empty, and broken.

If you are tired of trying to manufacture a self-energized light through religion that only looks similar to the real light of Christ, what happened to me needs to happen to you. Separate yourself from your religion, and pour whatever else is left into one of those little plastic communion cups. Hold it up to God and surrender to the broken and spilled-out life He has for you. You might want to pray something like this: "*Lord, there's nothing I can do to impress you. I need you. I know that I don't have anything that You need. Take my life and fill it with Yourself.*"

Get a small plastic communion cup. Keep it somewhere so that you can fill it with water every day. When it's filled, think of the list of things you try to fill your life with in order to measure up. Then pour it out. As you pour out the water, ask God to remind you today that all you need is the life of God living in you.

SEVEN

Light Switch

WHEN CHARACTER DISAPPEARS

In my church I grew up singing "This Little Light of Mine." It was a silly little tune that was the Sunday-school way of teaching us that we were to be lights for Jesus in a dark world. I grew up believing that this song was an evangelism metaphor. If I wanted to change the world, then I had to go and be light in the darkness.

To a lot of people, light has many different meanings. I grew up thinking that light was something pretty, something happy, something cute. "Won't let Satan *poof* it out...." Even now, when I hear light referenced in church, the picture is usually of somebody holding up a candle and telling us that we are a reflection of Jesus. Light seems to always be presented as a sentimental, emotional, devotional idea. But that imagery doesn't give justice to the vital role we play in bringing light into the world.

"Light" is the very life of God living inside us. Before Jesus left this earth, He said to His disciples, "*For a little while longer the Light is among you. Walk while you have the Light, so that darkness will not overtake you; he who walks in the darkness does not know where he goes. While you have the Light, believe in the Light, so that you may become sons of Light*" (John 12:35–36). In other words, when Jesus was about to leave the earth, He made sure His disciples knew that they were the light of the world. It was a cosmic version of "tag, you're it." Jesus declared that every person who genuinely places his or her dependence on His life becomes the light of the world.

The song is not just a little Sunday-school song; it's not meant to be a sentimental way to close out a concert or something to sing when we take up an offering. It is a literal declaration that every person who has come to know Jesus Christ personally has taken on the character of Christ. While we are in this world, we are the light. God has placed weight on our role in this world. Our role as bearers of His light is critical. Every moment of every day of every week of every year, we are the light of God in this world.

I could write all of the predictable things: "You are the light of the world. You need to be light and salt. You need to try to be a good person in the business world." But I know there is no possible way for you to ever value what it truly means to be the light until you see what life looks like when light is gone.

There are many believers who no longer place high value on the indwelling life of Christ. Other things have become more important, and they now pursue other values, other interests, and other things to fill up their lives. We all have been there at one time or another. Perhaps you are there now.

Somewhere, sometime, you bought into the idea that filling your life with other very important things was all right. Your intention was not to completely replace the light with other things. You never intended to make a complete switch. You still wanted the light in your life, but you also wanted there to be room for other things that you felt were just as important as the light. Sooner or later you moved out and let someone else shine where you once did. You said to yourself, "That's OK. After all, we are all part of the body of Christ. There are others who can take my place. These things in my life are really important. If they weren't, I wouldn't let them be a potential interference with the life of Christ in me."

The term *godly* is a reference to character. The godly man is a type of person. The godly man is the one who has taken on the persona of Christ. A switch was turned on in his character, which allows the character of Christ to begin to flow through him. The changes are evident to him and to others.

But somewhere along the way there is a light switch—a change in light. The godly man ceases to be. The man displaying the character of Christ changes; he switches. How is it that a godly person ceases to be? What changes? What is switched?

In Psalm 12 we read about David (the guy who killed Goliath and later became the king of Israel). In this Psalm, David was running from his son Absalom, who had initial success in overthrowing his father's kingdom. David's trusted friend and advisor Ahithophel had deserted David and joined forces with Absalom. While fleeing his home and city, David asked God for help because the advance of godless leadership in Israel had become greater than that of the godly. (Here's a curious note: Absalom's name means "giver of peace," and Ahithophel's name means "in their haste or folly." Abaslom was anything but a peacemaker, and Ahithophel was caught up in the haste and folly of Absalom's decision to attack his father.) Not only had David's son turned against him, but now David's most trusted advisor had denied the godly character that David had grown to depend on in him.

David's kingdom had been filled with success and victory. He was the bright spot in Israel's history. Everyone admired his family and advisors. But all of his glory began to crumble after he had an affair with his neighbor's wife.

Now David was homeless, his son and top advisor had betrayed him, he had lost his kingdom, and he had only a few moments to flee in order to save his life. The psalm he wrote at that time gives us a good look at what happens when believers choose to violate the character of Christ living inside them. When a light switch occurs, there are four consequences.

Chapter Seven

Position Compromised

Help, LORD, for the godly man ceases to be. (Psalm 12:1)

Choosing the light of Christ brings order into our lives. This light affects everything in and about us. Our priorities, our routines, and our relationships are all affected. Our place in life has been determined by our position in the Lord.

There are times when it seems easier just to disconnect from the pursuit of godliness and set our minds on something else. When we do, our position is compromised, and the godly man ceases to be. What once was light has switched to darkness.

We are all prone to compromise. In the morning when you're walking out the door to go to work and realize that you forgot to put on deodorant, what do you do? You don't go back and undress. You just go back and get the deodorant and jam it down your shirt. One button, and you're in! It's too much trouble to untuck and unbuckle because you're all situated. That's our nature. We're prone to find the shortcut. We are given to compromise. We tend to find what works at the moment. We're not going to go through all the big steps; we're just going to do what works for the moment. That's the nature of compromise.

Somewhere along the way of living the light, other things like achievement, affluence, success, and abundance become important. In the corporate culture, performance and promotion are the flagships of successful business. Financial independence and achievement become the goal, and if we're not careful, they become the focus of our hard work.

When this happens, it is only a small step to think, "Well, I'm a good person and I love God; but in order to achieve these things, I have to do some things that I know God is not going to approve of." What happens is our foundation gets switched. Instead of living out of our position in the Lord, a higher value is placed on success, achievement, and money. Character is traded for success. The position changes, and the godly man ceases to be.

Many have grown up in divorced homes because one of the parents let something become more important to them than the family. Take a man who loves God. At a certain stage in his life, he decides this whole God thing is not that important or that relevant for his life. So he decides to rebuild his life on success and money. When his wife and family get in the way of his success, divorce is not a problem. His foundation has been switched. He has made the decision that the things of God are not important anymore.

I watched a documentary once on people who go around blowing up abortion clinics in the name of God. There's something really wrong with that. I believe it's called hypocrisy! People are killing people who kill people. That doesn't make any sense, does it? These people are supposedly against abortion, yet they have no problem killing adults. They are for the lives of babies and against the lives of adults. I guess they figure that somebody who is in their eighty-first trimester has lived long enough, and it's time for them to go ahead and die. In the name of speaking up for the life of the unborn, they have chosen a course that clearly contradicts the character of God. God creates and supports life. He strictly prohibits murder by any means. The switch these people have made communicates to the world that the godly man ceases to be.

When we trade character for anything else, we have a light switch. We compromise our position. The godly man ceases to be.

Principles Held in Contempt

For the faithful disappear. (Psalm 12:1)

The faithful disappear because they quit living by the principles of God. The second consequence of a light switch is that we hold the principles of God in contempt; in other words, they no longer matter. Contempt is a chosen state of mind and a willful disobedience or disrespect for the principles of God. Contempt is a choice to no longer care. People who hold the principles of God in contempt are the ones who say, "Well, I just don't agree with that part of the Bible."

A pastor friend of mine has a daughter who is gorgeous and knows the things of God. She often sings in worship services and is planning on attending a Christian university. So naturally she's dating the anti-Christ, but she's hopeful he'll come around. She's utilizing the "flirt-to-convert" approach. I said to her, "I know you're familiar with the part of the Bible that teaches that light has no business with darkness. I'm not judging you; I just want to know how you get around that."

She said, "Well, I just don't agree with that part of the Bible."

What was I thinking? Of course she doesn't agree with that part of the Bible.

Isn't that what people do? They get out their big, black Bible-verse blotter and blot out all of the verses they don't agree with. Or they just make up their own New Testament and offer it alongside the real one on late-night cable.

When character is no longer our priority, we convince ourselves that our situation is different. "That part of the Scripture may be what's right for you, but it may not be what's right for me!" These are the symptoms of someone who is holding the principles of God in contempt.

Postmoderns have the reputation of being the most uncommitted generation of all time, and it shows up in our dating habits. It's not really called dating; it's called hanging out. Of course, it really is more than hanging out; it's some sort of relationship. But we don't like to define it as a relationship because if we define the relationship, that requires us to base our lives on some principles. And principles require that we apply character to the relationship. As long as there is no definition, as long as there are no principles, there needs to be no accountability. And because there is no accountability, there won't be any guilt when the breakup happens. We take the easy route. We say, "We're just hanging out." We make up our own rules in relationships.

Anytime we trade in character for the pursuit of something else, the principles of God are going to crowd our lifestyle. Our lifestyle will come face to face with the principles of God. Guess which one we'll reject?

We read the Bible and hear what it says. We know the principles of God, yet we say, "That's not my deal. That may be your thing, but it's not my thing. I just don't feel that's right for me." When we take this approach to God's principles, we literally dethrone God from our hearts. The principles of God have become subjective. We vote on them. We say, "If it doesn't make my life hurt too badly, I'll do it. If it doesn't take me out of my comfort zone, I'll do it."

Anytime we choose to live in opposition to the character of Christ in us, our position in God is compromised. The principles of God are held in contempt; they no longer shape our lives. We become our own god, and we make up our own rules.

What literally happens is we become practical atheists. We don't think of ourselves as atheists because we've grown up in God Land. Even though we have great pastors and sit under powerful preaching, we obey God when it's convenient. When it helps us, we go God's way. When it hurts us, we pull away.

There's probably no place where we hold the principles of God in contempt more than when we're behind the wheel of a car. The horn blowing, the evil words, the cruel gestures—and that's just getting out of the church parking lot. That's a silly example, but it's the truth. In our minds it's easy to make the switch from living as if God is not around one moment to living for Him when we need to the next. That's holding the principles of God in contempt. We're putting ourselves at the center of our world instead of keeping God at the center of our lives.

Presence Ceases

> *With our tongue we will prevail; our lips are our own; who is lord over us?* (Psalm 12:4)

The third consequence of a light switch is that the presence of God stops. This doesn't mean that God moves out of our lives. What it does mean is that we can no longer feel the presence of God. The arrogance of contempt keeps building until the question is asked, "Who is lord over me?" The answer is no one! That's because character has been sacrificed for something else.

After we have lived that way long enough, our hearts get hard. We get to where we can't feel God. We become calloused to conviction. We have been holding the principles of God in contempt for so long that almost nothing feels wrong.

This is why some people feel that eerie silence when they try to talk to God. They feel the silence indicating that something is not right. But their hearts have gotten hard, and now nothing breaks through. They aren't sorry for anything because they don't feel that they've done anything wrong. They have justified themselves for so long that no matter who speaks on God's behalf, the words just bounce off their hearts of stone and land somewhere else in the building.

God has a process He uses to keep us focused on living out of His character. It's called brokenness. It is inevitable that all of us have some hardness of the heart toward the things of God. By taking us to places and putting us in situations where we have to trust Him, He keeps us focused on His character. He does this so He can break through the hard parts of our hearts.

If your heart is hard, you have disconnected from the process of continued brokenness. When God tries to break you, you resist Him. When God brings you to the end of yourself, you fight it and won't give in. "It's my deal," you say. "It's my life. I don't feel that it's wrong." Your heart has become rock hard.

If you recognize that your heart is hardening but you choose to stay there, you will find that over time you will not feel the presence of God. You will find that you can't connect with Him. You will become hardened to the presence of God. Disconnected from God is a scary place to be. Once you become hardened to God's presence, you face the next consequence of a light switch.

Power Base Collapses

"Because of the devastation of the afflicted, because of the groaning of the needy, now I will arise," says the LORD; "I will set him in the safety for which he longs." (Psalm 12:5)

When your life has a light switch and regresses toward darkness, your power base collapses. When the power base of those who are light in the world collapses, the influence of light lessens. Light retreats and the darkness advances. The afflictions that attack people and the struggles of the needy in society increase as the credibility we have as sons and daughters of light decreases.

When our power base collapses, the wickedness of this world experiences undeserved victory. "*The wicked strut about on every side when vileness is exalted among the sons of men*" (Psalm 12:8). Let me say it another way: When the children of light exalt the vile things of darkness, we become responsible for the increase of affliction and neediness in the world. Let me say it a third way: The church, the body of God's light, is responsible for feeding the hungry, clothing the naked, housing the homeless, and relieving the afflictions of the world. The more light we live, the less our society will be afflicted. These problems are rampant because the godly man ceases to operate from a solid power base.

The answer to these problems is not more legislation or more tax dollars. There aren't enough dollars to fix these problems. We don't need more laws; the ones we have now aren't working. The answer to these problems is for the lights of the world to return to their eternal power base.

There are also needy and afflicted people within the church. I spoke at a men's retreat and met a lot of guys who were businessmen, entrepreneurs; both white- and blue-collar workers. I asked them what kind of reputation Christians have in the business world. They said to me, "It's a known fact that if businesses have a little fish on their business card or sign, that translates into, 'You're going to get slammed by this business. These people can't be trusted. They're going to rip you off and leave you high and dry.'"

This statement was made by Christian businessmen talking about how the world perceives Christians in business! The fish

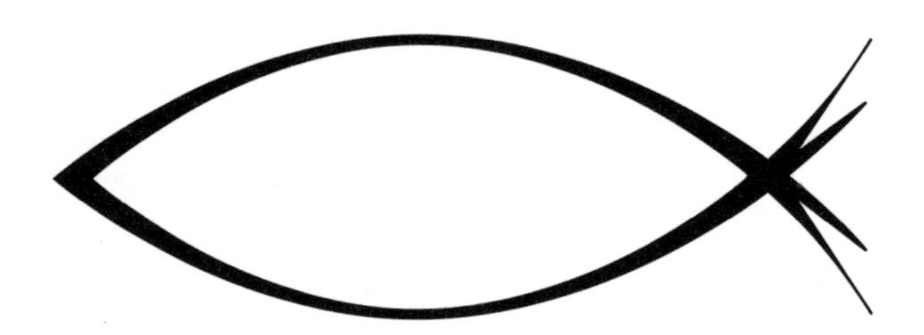

used to be a symbol of revolution painted on a doorpost with blood, symbolizing the fact that someone who lived there was a follower of Christ. It is unfortunate, but it only takes a few shady businessmen with fish on their cards to give the impression that any business bearing the symbol of the fish is untrustworthy.

I spoke in another place where I met a guy who had a life Hollywood could make a TV movie out of. He was worth millions of dollars, and he came to the Bible study in his Ferrari. This guy had reached a point in his life where things were so bad, he had put a gun in his mouth. He happened to have his radio tuned in to a Christian station at the time, and he heard that God loved him. He took the gun out of his mouth and prayed to receive Christ. He started attending the Bible study, where he found energy, great music—and everybody was sober (he'd never seen that before). He discovered that he could have a good time and still remember it the day after.

He was totally overwhelmed, but he kept coming back to the Bible study week after week. Even though he was extremely wealthy, he tried to make some friends and get involved. I went to lunch with him one day and asked him what he had discovered in his new God life. He said, "I discovered that Christian women are easier than women in the world. Christian women will do for free what I had to pay women in the world to do." I didn't know what to say. His words still break my heart.

Our power base has collapsed. We've lost credibility. The world looks at us and says, "These Christians want fame, money, success, power, and position. They want the same things we want."

Our power base springs out of character. When character is violated, credibility is lost. When character is switched for convenience, the power supporting the base we have stood on is gone. Anything we say or do is heard and seen with question marks surrounding it. Our power base is the only thing that makes us legitimate in the world.

Where are the lights? Where are the men and women of character? We've traded character in for something else. As a result, we've lost credibility with the people who need the light the most.

What are we to do now? How can we recapture our power base?

Personal Commitment

The answer is that we must return to the pursuit of character. I challenge every believer to look at his or her life and ask, "What am I really pursuing? What is it that is ordering my life? Is it the character of God, or is it something else?" We need to say to the Lord, "Whatever I have traded character for, I give it all away and return to You, Lord Jesus. I choose to realign myself to You."

God has a wonderful plan for your life. Jeremiah 29:11, 13 says, "*'For I know the plans that I have for you,' declares the* LORD*, 'plans for welfare and not for calamity to give you a future and a hope.... You will seek Me and find Me when you search for Me with all your heart.'*" God's message is restoration for you if you seek Him with all your heart. He will hear your prayer when it is spoken from a heart that completely seeks Him. His plans for your future and hope will be restored to you. Once again you will be able to walk confidently with your power base restored.

Perhaps you find yourself feeling convicted of encouraging the advance of darkness. Maybe you have been through the light switch and recognize that you have chosen something other than the real light of Christ. It could be that you have gone so far that you have no power base at your place of work or in your family or church. The good news about the light switch is that it can be switched back. Your light can be re-*lit*. You can reset your priorities and choose the real light of Christ over anything else. Your power base can be reconstructed. You can once again have real influence and power at work, in your family, and at church.

The return to the light of Christ begins with your decision to walk away from what you have chosen. Walk away from self-will, self-indulgence, and independence. Walk away from holding God's principles in contempt. It takes just as much energy to walk in darkness as it does to walk in the light. We all have to expend energy to live; why not make it productive instead of destructive?

If we are going to make a priority out of the pursuit of character, we must clearly see what it is we are pursuing. That's the focus of the next chapter.

Determine that every day for the next week, each time you turn on or off a light in a room, you will be reminded of your role as light in the world.

EIGHT

Lit List

CHARACTER IS...

Character is important to everybody. It's an intangible thing, but we can sense when people have it and when they don't. For instance...

If you get on an airplane and see that the pilot is wearing two different colored shoes, that's a bad sign. He may not be that great a pilot if he's not all that observant.

If you go to the doctor and he's wearing a Fisher Price stethoscope, that's cause for concern.

If your dentist has blood in his hair, keep your mouth closed.

If your dietitian is five-foot-four and weighs three hundred pounds, there might be room for a few questions.

If the faith healer has a toupee—well, if he can't make hair grow...

All these things are deal breakers. What's showing on the outside makes you wonder what's on the inside. We all grow up making a mental list of the characteristics we want in a perfect mate. Height, weight, hair color, hobbies, where they like to shop, how much money their parents have—you know the list. There are actually seminars that tell people to write down a list of qualities for their ideal mate. I've met people who have been to these seminars; some of them actually have three hundred things on their lists! There is no way they are going to meet anyone who fits all of their criteria. Anyway, if they have time to list three hundred things, they need to get out more often.

The reality is that as we get older, we mark some of those things off our lists. "Well, I guess I don't *have* to have that. Well, I guess that's not so important." Wait long enough and if you're still single, your list will have been whittled down to anyone who is breathing and has a day job.

When our lists are stripped down to the bare bones, we find that the one thing we are really looking for in a potential mate is character. Character matters to us. When we complain about our parents, our friends, or our coworkers, the thing we complain about most is a lack of character.

It's obvious when people lack character. When we get around them, we notice that there's an edge to their lives. Something doesn't ring true, and it makes them stand out from the rest of the world around them. Every one of us has been victimized at some time in our lives by someone who lacked character. We've been on the cutting end of a bad relationship. We've been on the painful end of a business deal; we've been ripped off and lied to. It's impossible to hide character, and it's impossible to hide the lack of it.

Can you define the *lit* life yet? We've said it before. You could log on to www.davetown.com and find out. But I'll make it easy and just tell you again: The *lit* life is *the life of God living in us*. The life of God is true character, and God ignites it within you. Apart from God, there is nothing within you that even resembles real character. You can no more start the character of God in your life than a candle can light itself.

Many of us have grown up without great character role models. Extreme rock stars and careless athletes are the characters that have replaced people with real character. When someone writes a book like this one encouraging us to be people of character, the message can sound like a morality statement: "Be moral. Improve your life." But that's not it.

Charisma Is Not Character

We live and work in a world where character is talked about but not rewarded. Our world rewards *charisma*, not character. Charisma is what turns a bald spot into a part. Business is more interested in how people look and how they "come off" in a meeting than in what's really underneath.

When someone's life is directed and controlled by charisma, everything is superficial. Charisma makes a lousy foundation because it's always in flux. A relationship with someone whose entire being is based on charisma is about as stable as a sandcastle on ice. Yet more relationships are built on charisma than character. Everything starts off great, but once the charisma wears off, so does the desire to stay in the relationship.

Charisma requires some effort to develop, but it's easier to develop than character. Character exists within the person before it shows up on the outside. Genuine character actually produces its own charisma; however, manufactured charisma does not produce character.

Focusing on the development of charisma can actually weaken and undermine the development of the character of Christ in the life of an individual. At the same time, a focus on the development of character produces an appropriate amount of charisma in that life. Individuals focused on developing charisma are more concerned with their image and how people perceive them. Individuals focused on developing character are more interested in doing what's right. They know that people's perceptions are of less importance and significance than genuine character. To put it another way, they have greater respect for what God knows about them than what other people perceive about them.

Look at the following illustration. Charisma is black, and character is white. In the person concerned mainly with charisma, development of character is confined to a small portion of life and may or may not be deemed very important. In the individual absorbed with the development of character, however, charisma takes its natural place as the thin outer shell that can be observed by others.

Chapter Eight

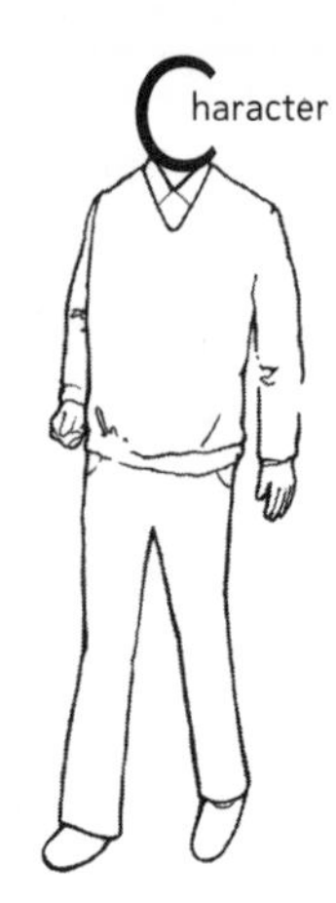

One time after speaking on the subject of character, I talked with a man who was the CEO of a good-sized company and who had some downsizing decisions to make. He didn't realize it, but he was caught up in making sure that his decisions made him look good. He confessed to me that he wanted to make the right decisions but was having a tough time doing it. He knew what was best for the ultimate health of the company, but he just couldn't make the decisions. I listened and then compassionately asked him, "Bro, do you want to look good, or do you want to make a difference?" His silence told us both that he was more concerned with how he looked than what was right.

I want to let the Bible define for itself what real character is. Psalm 15 is a psalm about character. It tells us five things that define our understanding of illuminating, world-changing character. In the opening verse David asks the question, "*O Lord, who may abide in Your tent? Who may dwell on Your holy hill?*" What David wants to know is: Who gets to hang out with God?

In Old Testament times the place of worship was divided into an outer court, an inner court, and something called the "holy of holies." The holy of holies was the place of intimacy with God, and only certain people were allowed in that little room. David is asking God, "Who is the person who gets to be in that little room where you are?"

David desires an intimate relationship with God, and he acknowledges that character is the prerequisite for that relationship and all relationships. In this psalm he shows us five aspects of real character.

Prerequisite for Authentic Relationships

> *O Lord, who may abide in Your tent? Who may dwell on Your holy hill? He who walks with integrity, and works righteousness…* (Psalm 15:1–2)

Who gets to be close to God? The answer is the people who have made the character of God their focus. Genuine character is the very life of God. David is telling us that the people who get in, the people who have the intimate relationship with God, are the ones who are pursuing the life of God. They are committed to having their lives conformed, bent, and shaped around the life of God.

Any relationship built without character will always be superficial because it is built on an image without anything to back it up. The same is true for our relationship with God. In fact, character is a prerequisite for every one of our relationships: our parents, our friends, our coworkers, whom we date, and whom we marry. Character is the thing that makes relationships work.

Character is the true test of every relationship. Two people who seem suited for each other may be compatible in many ways, but if one of those two people lacks character, that relationship will self-destruct. Every relationship has trouble over time, but character is the bonding agent that keeps it together.

This is also true in the business world. If we enter into an agreement with someone who lacks character, in one way or another we're going to get burned. That person doesn't operate based on the same business values we do. He or she could twist off and hurt us, the business, or both at any time.

It's dangerous to decide whom we will marry based on how a person looks. We don't marry anatomy; we marry character. Later in life, when wrinkles have replaced the smooth skin, all we'll be left with is the life of God in that person.

Character should be a prerequisite for all of our relationships.

Personal Reinvention

...and speaks truth in his heart. (Psalm 15:2)

We're a nation that has spent so much time looking in the mirror at the outside, we've forgotten to look on the inside. Health clubs are more crowded than most airline flights I take. America has lost its soul, so it focuses on its body. "If you can't feel good," the thinking goes, "then you might as well look good." The result is that we have a lot of beautiful, hollow people walking around.

David identifies the source for character as the inside of us, the heart. We have been told for years that Christians do or don't do certain things. Depending on whom we listen to, the list varies. But changing our image outside without changing our character inside is going about it backward. Character is more than how we act; it's who we are.

Pursuing morality apart from the life of God is always frustrating. True morality is the outward expression of our inward character. If our inward values are not built upon the life of God within us, any morality we manufacture will end up in frustration and failure. We may be able to disguise the failure and hide it from others, but inside we won't be able to ignore it.

At the moment we receive Christ, our spirits are brought to life, but our minds, instincts, hungers, and drives are still the same. God places the Spirit of Jesus Christ inside us, and He begins to go to work invading our thought life, our instincts, our hungers, and our drives. He works in each of us in His own time for His own pleasure and will. We are in a process of reinvention! This is an internal process done by an internal God. We may be waiting for lightning and thunder, but God is at work reshaping our lives from the inside out.

Our part of the strategy of reinvention is to join God in the process of change. We need to look for what God is already doing inside of us and ask to be a part of that. We can pray a simple prayer: "God, form my life, shape my life, and let my desires desire what You desire. Let what turns you on turn me on. God, let what breaks Your heart break my heart."

As God begins to answer this prayer, the life of Christ will begin to spread through us like wildfire. It is God doing the work inside us. His answer continues to come in response to our confession: "Lord Jesus, I didn't start this fire; You did. And I can't stoke it; You have to. All I've done is open up my life, and You stepped out of heaven and into my heart. Now You've gone to work on my soul. If I am to have character, You have to reinvent me from the inside out."

Rebellion and self-indulgence slow down the process. They fly in the face of what God wants to do in us. Reinvention requires cooperation with the inner workings of God in our lives. Rebellion is a stiff arm in the face of God. Self-indulgence is gorging ourselves on anything that makes us not hungry for the things of God.

Look for the places where God is already at work in you. Ask Him to melt your heart into His and give you the grace to cooperate fully with Him. Reinvention is a lifelong process. You will always be under renovation, and the next chapter will help you understand the elements of change that God is bringing to bear on your life.

Predetermined Response

The biggest problem we face in character development is not the problems we face. The biggest problem we face is that we haven't predetermined what our responses will be to those situations. If we stop and think about it, we can write a fairly complete list of the problems we face or will face in the future. If we can write a list of the problems, then we should be able to predetermine how we will respond to each of these situations. It will take some thought...but it will take even more *courage* to live out.

In the moment a problem hits, we typically seek the advice of whoever is closest to us. We go with whatever is easy or popular. We float through, doing whatever feels right or is the least painful or least challenging. This is not character.

Character is a predetermined response. Character is agreeing with God beforehand on how we are going to act. A person of character says, "I don't need to know the details of the situation. I've already agreed with God in my heart that I'm going to respond in such a way that it honors the life of God in my heart." That is character!

How can we possibly know the right thing to do in every situation even before we are faced with it? We can't. But don't worry about that. Most of the problems we will face are fairly obvious, and so are the correct character-building responses.

The rest of Psalm 15 is a list of predetermined responses to some of the more obvious situations we all face. I call it my *Lit List*. David lays out eight predetermined responses of a person who lives by character. The danger in my listing these for you is that it can appear that I'm handing you a list of things to do. I am not giving you such a list. These are some of the core values that God would have all of us drive deeply into our hearts. These core values will help you see what God's Word has to say about predetermined responses to life situations.

These eight responses are given with the understanding that they are to be done out of a wholehearted pursuit of the life of God. If you do these apart from the life of God, there is no guarantee that they will work. This is not a list of things for you to do better and try harder. This is a predetermination of a course of action that says you are going to pursue the life of God with everything within you.

Psalm 15 lists eight predetermined responses for people of character.

1. They Do Right

In verse 2, David says that people of character work *righteousness*. That means that they do the right thing. And doing the right thing means that they do God's thing God's way, no matter how great the cost. David's life is a testimony that no matter how costly it may feel at the moment, the character developed by doing right is far more priceless.

2. They Deal with Their Mistakes

Verse 2 also says that people of character *walk with integrity*. That means their external matches their internal. They are the same on the inside as they are on the outside. Being people of integrity doesn't mean they've never made a mistake. They just have owned up to it, faced it, and made corrections.

I have five guys in my life who are my "life covenant" guys. They make sure I stay on track. They are all older than I am, and they all have checkered pasts. One guy lost his business and got it back. Another guy lost his marriage but restored it. These guys have records, but they are the godliest men I know. That's not because they are perfect but because they have dealt with their mistakes; they have owned up to them rather than making excuses. These guys have faced their failures and triumphed.

Some companies perform extensive background checks before hiring someone. Everyone has mistakes in his past that he wishes no one would ever know about. People of character have dealt with these things and can honestly say, "That's right. I did those things, but I took care of it. I brought closure to it." People of character deal with their mistakes.

3. They Delight in Honesty

In verse 2, David says that people of character *speak truth in their hearts*. This means that they take delight when things are genuine and honest. People of character ferociously guard the honesty of their hearts. They know that everything flows out of their hearts and that if their hearts are not filled with truth and honesty, their lives will reflect the void.

These days people don't have to be guilty—just accused. An accusation can ruin a life more quickly than actual, hard evidence. "Sleepovers" are the big thing these days. A couple goes out on a date to dinner and a movie. They plan on going to the lake early the next morning. When they get home from the movie, it's after midnight. So he sleeps over at her house. She sleeps in her bed; he sleeps on the couch. Nothing happens. Nothing goes on. It is just easier for him to sleep there since they have to get up early the next day.

The problem with this is that it doesn't have the appearance of honesty. The entire situation looks less than honorable and can compromise a person's reputation for honesty and character.

If someone approaches you with a lucrative business deal that would require you to be dishonest, what would you do? Some of us would ask, "How much dishonesty is involved?" as if dishonesty can be measured in ounces and pounds. But it is impossible to mix dishonesty with the honest character of Christ.

People of character have predetermined for themselves that honesty will rule their hearts. The honesty they have chosen actually helps them see the subtle things that could compromise their character.

4. They Discipline Their Words

Verse 3 says, "*He does not slander with his tongue.*" Can this be any clearer? For many of us, our greatest hang-up is our mouths. This is not news to any of us. We sit down at a table with some of our friends, and the soup du jour is crème de la cutdown.

I'm always on the road traveling, so many times I eat alone. Since I have nothing else to do at the restaurant, I listen to other people talk. I can't believe what people talk about. They complain about everything from their bosses to the people at the rental car desk. Much of their conversation is just nitpicky, gossipy, backbiting, slanderous stuff.

These are the kinds of words that harden our hearts toward the presence of God. Using them doesn't make God any less God, but it makes it harder for us to know what He's doing in us. This is why the Bible makes it a point to say that "*death and life are in the power of the tongue*" (Proverbs 18:21). We have the ability to bring about death in our own souls and in the souls of others by our words.

What happens when people in your cubicle village (or whatever you call those little places where you work) engage in gossip, backbiting, and slander, and you can't get away from it? If you're a person of character, that's predetermined. You don't open your mouth. You just close your mouth and back out. Words have power, and so does silence. Part of disciplining your words is knowing not only what to say but when to say it and when to shut up.

5. They Defend the Righteous

In verse 4, David says people of character *honor those who fear the Lord*. That means that if a guy at your job is a believer and he comes under attack for his faith, you come to his defense. It doesn't matter if you are personal friends with him or not; he serves the same God. Church and denominational tags are irrelevant. The point is that both of you serve the same God and belong to the same kingdom. When people in the kingdom come under fire, you've got to go to their aid regardless of the cost.

It may cause you to lose standing in the eyes of your friends; it may cause people to talk about you. If you are in line for a promotion, taking a stand for the Christian under attack could jeopardize your opportunities. It doesn't matter, because defending the righteous is part of pursuing the life of God.

6. They Deliver the Goods

Verse 4 says, "*He swears to his own hurt and does not change*." This means that when people of character say yes, they mean yes. When they say no, they mean no. It's not "kind of," "sort of," "maybe I could."

When you sign up to bring a Dr. Pepper to the get-together, you bring it. That's delivering the goods. You don't say, "I forgot. Sorry." If you make a commitment to go to a retreat or to participate in an event, show up! That's what it means to deliver the goods.

What we often give is a partial yes: "Sure, unless something better comes along." "You bet, unless I get a bigger, better deal." "Yeah, unless I'm inconvenienced by it." That's not character. Character is the predetermined response that if you agree to do something, you're going to follow through with it.

Guys, if you have a pickup truck and you tell some friends that you'll help them move, show up. If you don't want to help people move, sell the truck. People with pickup trucks always get used. Hey, it's free! But if you say you're going to do it, be there. People of character come through. They can be counted on. They're consistent. They're predictable. 'Nuf said.

7. They Distribute Their Wealth

I know you're thinking "If I had any." Verse 5 says, "*He does not put out his money at interest.*" What David is talking about is how people of character use their money. People of character distribute their wealth. They don't use it only for themselves. They have not bought into the myth of ownership. They understand that they didn't get what they have on their own; it is all a gift from God. And if everything is a gift from God, then everything needs to be used to accomplish God's purposes on this earth.

People of character see their paychecks as opportunities to make a lasting impact on the world around them. They will still pay rent and buy gas, groceries, and clothes; but what they buy, where they buy it, and how much they pay for it is impacted by their underlying commitment to use everything to advance the kingdom of God.

Business pressures and godly character frequently collide. Nevertheless, business decisions must be made, and some of these decisions involve layoffs, pay cuts, raises, responses to unethical conduct, and ways to make money. What we must learn is that these decisions are more about who we are in our character than who we are in our organization. We must see every business decision for what it is: a character decision that has an effect on our business.

Somehow God has put you in the right company. He got you your job. Everything you've done that has been successful can be traced back to the hand of God. People of character realize this and take at least ten percent of their income and put it back into the work of God. They realize the importance of helping a church, supporting a missionary, or assisting somebody who is in need. Their response is predetermined.

8. They Do Not Use Others

Verse 5 continues, *"Nor does he take a bribe against the innocent."* People of character don't use people; they use things. They don't use people to meet their emotional, physical, or financial needs. People belong to God. People of character treat everyone as though they were sons and daughters of God, not as though they were there to serve their purposes. It's predetermined.

When we serve and honor others by placing their needs above our own, we actually assist them in reaching their goals. When we view others as children of God, we treat them in ways that help them move one step closer in the process of knowing Jesus Christ. If we are people of character, it's predetermined. We treat people with godly respect.

Passions Revealed

Funny thing about life: Our passions show up in our lives. Passions are the things that we will do almost anything for. Another way to define passions is "core values." Core values are observable behaviors. It's not accurate for us to call something a core value or a passion if it's not an observable behavior in our lives.

In Psalm 15 David tells us about his passion for an intimate relationship with God. The good news is that his life reflected that passion. First Samuel 13:14 says that David was a man after God's own heart. Anyone looking at David's life could see that he was passionate about keeping his relationship with God intimate.

Take a moment and read the following list. It is a list of the eight predetermined responses we've just talked about. I have personalized them to make a point. As you read them, ask yourself: *Which of these eight responses do I need the most help with?*

1. I do the right things.
2. I deal with my mistakes instead of hiding from them.
3. I deal honestly and truthfully with everyone and in everything.

4. I am careful to use my words to build life in myself and others.
5. I defend the righteous when they are unrighteously accused.
6. I do what I say I will do.
7. I use my resources to build up the kingdom of God.
8. I do not use others to accomplish my own agenda.

Now take another moment and ask God which of these eight predetermined responses *He* thinks you need the most help with.

If these eight things were printed on a card and given to your best friend to rate you, how would your best friend rate you? If the card was given to your spouse and your spouse was asked to honestly rate you on these eight things, what would he or she say? If your children were asked to tell how they rate you on these eight things, would you be proud or shamed? How would your boss rate you?

I've heard this story several times over the past three years. Imagine a one-hundred-twenty-foot I-beam. An I-beam is a piece of steel used in constructing buildings and bridges that is shaped like the capital letter *I*. The flat edges are usually about six inches wide. If I put that I-beam on the flat surface of a parking lot and asked you to walk the length of it for one hundred dollars, would you do it? Sure, easy hundred bucks. What if I took that same I-beam and put it at the top of and in between two tall buildings? Would you walk the beam for the same hundred bucks? No? How about for a thousand? No? How about for a million dollars? No? What if someone held your child over the edge of the building and told you that if you didn't walk the beam, he would drop your child? Feel the passion? Passion makes the difference in what we really value. If the beam were over thirteen hundred feet off the ground, what would you be passionate enough to walk it for?

The cost of developing godly character is high, but the life it yields is priceless. David lets us know that God makes Himself intimate with godly people. I pray that you will choose to make these eight things your own passion. Make them core values that truly are observable in your life. If you do, your life will be unsinkable.

Presiding Resilience

Godly character brings with it the ability to bounce back. David closes Psalm 15 by saying, "*He who does these things will never be shaken.*" This is the concluding promise of the psalm. God gives the ability to bounce back to those people who choose to pursue the presence of the life of God. This presiding resilience is why the Bible says that when a righteous man falls, "*he will not be hurled headlong, because the LORD is the One who holds his hand*" (Psalm 37:24).

There is resilience when God is holding your hand. You will fall. But when you do, you fall forward. When you make a mistake, you make it in pursuit of the life of God. When you fall, it's not fatal. When you fail, it's not final, because God pulls you out of it.

I led a Bible study in Houston, Texas, years ago. God had brought one of the study's leaders out of hard-core drug use. There was no question in the mind of anyone in leadership that he was walking with God. For whatever reason, one weekend he relapsed. He called one of the other leaders and told him that he needed help. He said, "I knew I shouldn't have done it, but I did." He had enough character to pick up the phone and say, "I need your help." The leadership came beside him and defended him because he was one of the righteous who was in need. He made his mistakes, he worked his way through them, and now he's back in leadership. He got his life and his future back. Why? Because God was in his life. He had been *lit* by the life of God. He had cooperated with God and built into his life the predetermined responses for just such a time. When the time came, he knew what to do, and he had the courage to do it.

The goal of this chapter has been to help you see the big picture of character. Throughout the next few chapters, we'll slice up this big picture and take some closeup looks at some of character's finer points.

Write out the eight predetermined responses from this chapter. Put the list in a place where you can read it for ten straight days. If you really have courage, ask a good friend to rate you on the eight responses.

NINE
Direct Light

THE ONLY WAY TO TRULY CHANGE CHARACTER

The computer craze is out of control. It won't be long before people will be saying, "Books? Paper? What are those?" I'm happy to say I am nowhere near the cutting edge of technology—I'm on the blunt corner. I still haven't mastered Pong.

Our world has become overly dependent on technology and enamored with tech toys. We have pagers with flip-out keyboards, cell phones with Internet access, palm devices with MP3 players. Whatever would we do without the ability to get the latest-to-the-nano-second shopping, sports, and entertainment news? (I believe it's called a newspaper. Look into it.)

Cars now have GPs, or "global positioning" computers. They come complete with full-color maps and an automated voice that calls out directions in five different languages. Hey, I'm not Columbus in search of uncharted territory. I'm only going to the 7-Eleven and back home. I don't need a computer to tell me where the Slurpees are.

Besides, if technology is so great, why can't I keep a cell phone signal and turn my head at the same time?

I'm a low-tech person living in a hi-tech world. Even as I write this book, I'm not sitting at a PC doing the edit-cut-and-paste clicks. Oh no, every page is painstakingly handcrafted for you, the reader, because I love you. And I have never lost anything that I've downloaded to paper.

The frustration for me with the new technology frontier is that it changes so quickly. No matter what I purchase, by the time I carry it out of the store, it's a Beta player.

"Oh, but technology is wonderful." That's what people say. Then why is the whole world ruled by the same sound: a busy signal?

My insecurity about personal computing is heightened when my lack of computer savvy becomes unbelievably obvious to my friends' kids. These seven-year-olds speak to me in a condescending tone, like the host of *Weakest Link*. I'm not proud of my ignorance. But it has kept me from having to learn the new vocabulary of PCs. Take the word "RAM," for instance. I've always thought RAM is what took the place of Isaac on the altar. RAM is also a driving maneuver, one that I use often. "Hard drive" is going back home after my girlfriend has told me she doesn't want to see me anymore. "Clicking the mouse" is the sound of a rodent getting slammed in a trap.

One useful term I learned from my journey through Tech Land is "POP." That's short for "point of presence." The POP is a place where connection is made possible through a collection of modems and routers. Their function is to pick the best route by which to send information. They insure that all the data arrives at its destination at the right time.

POP is vital in developing and deepening the character of Christ in us. In Scripture, the "point of presence" is the place where all growth and change takes place in our lives. It's the place where God sees to it that all that is real in Christ is made real in us.

The terms for POP in the Old Testament are "refuge," "fortress," or "dwelling place." David often used these words in writing the Psalms. He called God his protector, his fortress, and his strength.

The New Testament translation for the POP process is "abiding." To abide means to hang out with God. It literally means to be attached to God. We are told to hang out with God and let Him do the changing in us from the inside out.

Abiding Orientates

> *Abide in Me, and I in you. As the branch cannot bear fruit of itself unless it abides in the vine, so neither can you unless you abide in Me.* (John 15:4)

The beginning of abiding is God's stepping out of heaven and into our lives. He does the stepping. He comes into us. At our invitation He sets up His home in our hearts. He abides in us and invites us to abide with Him. The God of the universe chooses to answer our request and come into us. Then He invites us to hang out with Him.

When God abides in us and we abide in Him, He produces three things in us that literally change the way we live.

1. He Produces Ultimate Freedom

Most Christians spend their lives trying to produce fruit for God. We volunteer time, give money, and do ministry projects that we hope will produce something beneficial for the kingdom of God. The problem is that while our motivation may be right, our efforts usually end up having a smaller than desired impact. We have great plans and desires, but the results never seem to measure up.

God never expects us to produce fruit. We are the vines; He is the branch. We are supposed to bear the fruit; He does the producing. But that can only happen when we are abiding in Him. The reason our Christian lives have so little fruit is that we do so little abiding.

In the Old Testament, the temple was lighted by lamps. These lamps were designed to look like branches originating out of a central vine. Each branch was carved and had on it a representation of fruit, and that's where the flame was. The oil for the lamps represented the Holy Spirit, and it flowed from the vine out to the branches and produced the light. Notice that in this picture, "abiding" and "light" are vividly connected.

When I was a young man, I spent nearly two years of my life asking God what He wanted me to do. I remember begging Him to just let me know what He expected from me. I was willing to do anything, go anywhere, and be anything He wanted me to be. During that time all I heard from God was, "Love Me." Every time I read the Scripture, it seemed He was telling me, "Love Me."

Finally I got it and just began to focus on loving Him. It wasn't long before I saw the fruit He was beginning to produce in my life. I realized that God wanted me to hang out with Him and not worry about what kind of fruit my life would produce. If He had told me about the fruit, I would have tried to produce it without Him. His presence in my life gave me ultimate freedom from the pressure to produce anything for Him.

2. He Produces Uninterrupted Fellowship

The goal of abiding is for us to plug ourselves into God. He recreated us to have such a complete fellowship with Him that His life flows through every facet of our lives.

Think of everything we face in life as pearls. Each one is unique and potentially valuable. Abiding puts these experiences in direct connection with the life of God living in us. It's very similar to a strand of pearls in which the string runs through every pearl and holds the strand together. Each pearl depends on the string for security. And it is the string that allows the pearls to find continuity and ultimate beauty. Abiding is threading God's eternal resources through the separate events of our lives. It is making each event dependent on the life God brings to the situation. When we abide in Him, all of life's events take on the shared power of the abiding presence of God, and they clearly demonstrate His glory.

3. He Produces Unlimited Fruit

God has unlimited eternal resources, and He is capable of producing in our lives as much as He needs of anything that advances His kingdom.

Do you remember going to your grandma's house and seeing the bowl of plastic fruit on the kitchen table? From a distance the fruit looked real. But pick it up, and you knew immediately that it was fake. Trying to produce fruit ourselves may make us look good to others, but when they get close enough to our lives, they will see that it's all about us and not the fruit. God produces real fruit in real lives when the relationship with Him is built on abiding.

Understanding the process God uses for change and our role in that process is the focus of this chapter. The goal is to give you a better understanding of the rationale behind this journey called "character development." Basically, character is developed in the context of two critical relationships. The first is with God, and the second is with the people in our lives.

Our relationship with people does not produce the kind of lasting change that comes through our relationship with God. People influence us, but they don't necessarily bring about changes in our character. God places His character within us and sets about the task of working it into every part of our lives. Our relationship with God is the channel for real life change.

It helps to think of ourselves and the development of character in terms of a cross. The vertical arm of the cross is our relationship with God, and the horizontal arm is our relationship with others. We are influenced through our relationship with others, but real change comes through our relationship with God.

The frustrations of living the Christian life come when we focus more on our relationship with others than we do on our relationship with God. When we are more focused on relating well with people, we inevitably begin to look to them for direction. Somehow we forget that they, too, are dealing with the same frustrations of life and are looking outside themselves for direction.

Why has spiritual growth been such a struggle for so many for so long? We have literally put the cross on its side, making the horizontal arm function as the vertical arm. We misuse our relationship with others and look to them for the kind of leadership that will produce internal change. We put them in the position of God. Instead of relying on Him to work out His character through us, we expect others to tell us what to do in order to produce the change within ourselves.

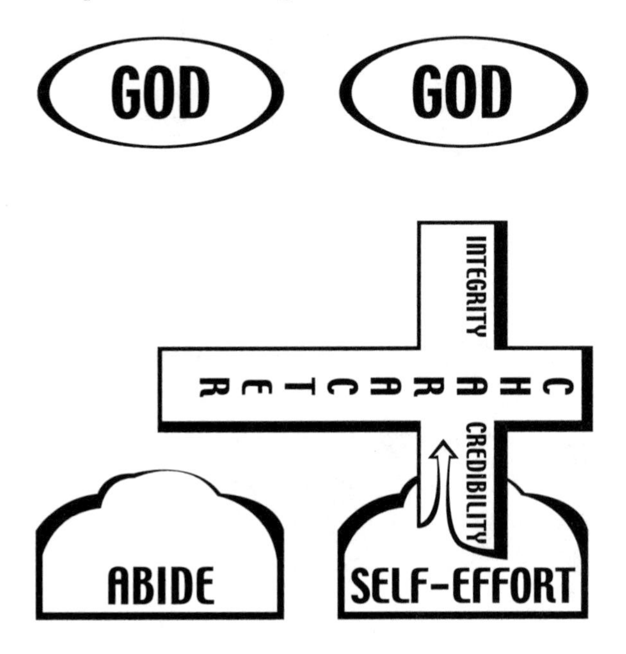

When the cross is on its side, it is pulled off its abiding foundation. No longer is there a direct link to God for the source of life and character. Now self-effort is the foundation, and morality becomes the source and the measure for character. God has been completely removed from the character equation. As long as the cross is on its side, genuine character development ceases.

The horizontal arm that should carry the overflow of God's life inside us is turned vertical and expected to fulfill a role it is incapable of. Instead of carrying this overflow into our relationships, it is now expected to connect us to God's character. Changing behavior to reflect greater integrity through self-effort becomes the natural substitute for character development. The result is an increase in religion and personal frustration.

This problem is as old as the Pharisees. They were the masters of religion. They focused completely on outward behavior as the source of inward change. Jesus referred to them as "blind guides" leading the blind (Matthew 15:14). Today religion has changed its name, but the focus remains the same: rigid adherence to a moral code or a set behavior in hopes of a change in character. Religion has turned the cross on its side.

The opposite of character is religion. The opposite of developing the character of Christ is becoming religious. Have you ever wondered where we fall when we fall from grace? We fall to religion. We fall back to changing our behavior. When we fall, we fall into the trap of becoming more concerned with preserving integrity and credibility before others than with preserving character. Do you see the pride? The focus is on how people respond to us rather than how we respond to God. People and their impression of us become more important than what God knows about us. We would rather change ourselves to please others than allow God to change us to please Him.

We have to put the focus of character development where it should be: on our relationship with God. In order for us to make progress in the Christian life and experience lasting change, we have to turn the cross right side up.

When the cross is turned to its correct position, all the parts work together. Imagine that the cross is an illustration of a person. When God enters a person, that's represented by the life of God being poured into the empty cross. The life of God begins to collect and rise toward the top, ultimately spreading horizontally through relationships and actions. In other words, the life of God changes us from the inside out. The change God produces is godly character, and it is manifested in two ways: *integrity* (how we do things) and *credibility* (our standing in the eyes of other people).

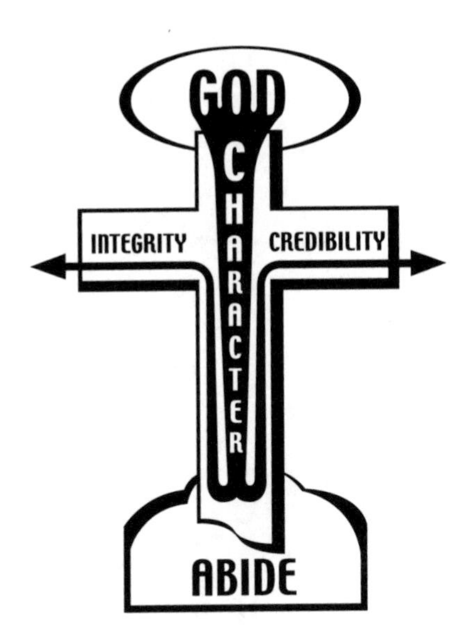

Many people in the Christian and secular worlds have substituted integrity for character. Proverbs 11:3 says, "*The integrity of the upright will guide them.*" Notice that the emphasis of this verse is on "the upright." It is the upright life that has the integrity that will guide it. The upright life is the one that has the character of God living in it. What this verse tells us is that integrity literally springs out of the character of God. Integrity is the demonstration of character. Uprightness forms the basis of our lives. Integrity does not bring about character; it merely expresses it.

Both integrity and credibility are observable expressions of true character. Any of us can temporarily change our behavior and make it look different from our true character. But we can't disguise lack of character with temporary behavior forever. Sooner or later true character shows itself. Temporary changes in behavior usually end up causing us more trouble than they took to manufacture. The result is a life that lacks credibility, consistency, and favor with others. "*The righteousness of the blameless will smooth his way*" (Proverbs 11:5). God's life living in us is blameless and produces righteousness in us. As His righteousness is consistently fleshed out in us, our credibility with people is increased.

Until a person's character is changed, it is pointless to deal with conduct and behavior. There is only one way to change morality and behavior, and that is through character. Trying to change conduct before character has been the fatal mistake of religion and society since the Garden of Eden.

We need to see and understand how God works in our lives:

> *For it is God who is at work in you, both to will and to work for His good pleasure. Do all things without grumbling or disputing; so that you will prove yourselves to be blameless and innocent, children of God above reproach in the midst of a crooked and perverse generation, among whom you appear as lights in the world.* (Philippians 2:13–15)

This passage tells us there are five keys to how God works His character in and through us.

The Arena of Operation

> *For it is God who is at work* in you. (Philippians 2:13)

God goes to work inside us. Notice the words carefully: "It is God who is at work *in* you." God works on the inside. Cough medicine works on the inside. Rub the syrup on your arm, and you'll still have a cough (although insects will like you more). God is an inside God. He knows that the outside is designed to mirror the work He does on the inside.

The reason many people struggle with becoming a Christian is that they think they will be asked to change their behavior. People always ask, "If I give my life to Christ, do I have to stop smoking, drinking, sleeping around?" More often than not, they are told, "Yes." For some reason we go right for behavior modification.

Behavior is not where God begins the change. He doesn't start with how we appear or act. He doesn't start with the addiction or the problem; He starts with us. God's arena of operation is inside of us. He goes to work on our souls; He goes to work on our spirits. The arena of God's operation is internal.

Anyone who has been addicted knows that taking the behavior away does not change the controlling desires. But God goes to work on the drive inside. He goes to work on the thing that makes us want whatever it is we are addicted to. The change takes place not on the surface, behavioral level but on the internal, character level. If you've been struggling with something for years, you need to begin to pray, "God, change my appetite. Change my desire for this thing."

I have a friend who is now a minister. Before coming to Christ he was hooked on crystal meth (not the techno band...the drug). This addiction literally controlled his entire life. I asked him how he got into such a destructive drug. He said, "I needed it. My life hurt so much, and I was so sad. It was the only thing that evened me out." He explained that just like everyone else who has turned to a substance to make life better, the only time he felt good was while he was high or about to get high.

Here's the good news. My friend told me, "When I finally understood that Jesus was a person and He wanted to place His life in me—when I finally connected with the life of Christ—I lost my desire and my taste for the drugs." That is how change happens. God changed my friend's life, then his appetites and attitudes toward his addiction were changed. As a result the behavior, the craving for the drug, and the other destructive actions that go with drug abuse took care of themselves.

Some of us have been struggling because we've had the cross on its side. We've been trying to change our external behavior. We have been trying to quit, go cold turkey, and promise God that we are never going to do it again. That is not the answer. When God goes to work, He goes to work on the inside. His arena of operation is always internal.

Activity Is Ongoing

It is God who is at work *in you.* (Philippians 2:13)

The phrase "is at work" means that God is constantly at work in us. He is at work on Sundays and Wednesdays and while we're at retreats. He is at work every moment of every day of our lives. All the way through our lives, the thread that hooks every circumstance of life together is God's developing His character in us.

The word *work* literally means "to work in, to be active, to effectively produce." How many times have we thought of all the things we can do for God? This verse tells us that God is at work for us, producing something we cannot hope to produce: His character in us.

We live in a world where people throw in the towel on a marriage without really thinking about the consequences their actions will have on themselves and the kids. It's all about their own happiness and comfort. People use people to get ahead in business and then ruthlessly throw them aside to take the next step. It's all about their goals and accomplishments. We enter most relationships expecting them to dissolve. We just aren't sure how long it will take them to fall apart.

This is the same way we approach our relationship with God. We never expect God to stay with us through all the mistakes we will make in life. No other relationship seems to last that long. Sooner or later we disappoint everyone in our lives. We tend to compare our relationship with God to our human relationships. The truth is, every human relationship we have pales in comparison to the love relationship God has with us.

God established a love relationship with you when Jesus died on the cross. That was the outward demonstration of His commitment to never stop loving you. He is God, and before you were ever born, He knew everything you would ever say, think, or do. When Jesus took your sin on Himself, you hadn't committed one single sin, yet God knew what your sins were going to be. He knew you would choose to love someone else or something else more than Him, and yet He gave His son to die for you. He can't take back the death of Jesus, and He can't take back His commitment to love you and to build His character into your life.

Once God enters a life, He's there forever. He sets up His dwelling place there. He begins the process of developing His character in that life. He is constantly about the ongoing work of building His character in that person.

We must understand that change happens in our vertical relationship with God. Through every circumstance, through every event, through every relationship, God is working to bring about His change. There is not an event or a moment when God is not working His character into us.

Aim Is Obedience

> *Do all things without grumbling or disputing...* (Philippians 2:14)

None of us likes to be told what to do. But there are a lot of times when we have to bend our will to do what someone else tells us to do. We'd like to think that we always have a great attitude when that happens, but we don't.

Earlier in Philippians 2, Paul lets us see obedience in the life of Jesus: "*Being found in appearance as a man, He humbled Himself by becoming obedient to the point of death, even death on a cross*" (verse 8). Jesus spent His life asking the question, "What does God want?" Whatever drives us becomes the focus of our lives. Jesus was driven by obedience to God.

God changes us so that we will be able to obey Him without grumbling or disputing (either aloud or silently). The aim is for us to begin to live like Christ. While Jesus was on the earth, He said, "I only do what I see My Father doing. I don't invent My own stuff to do. Whatever God does, that is what I am doing." Do you know what that is? That's obedience. Think of the life Jesus lived. He left a perfect heaven where He had never known want or need. He came to earth, and He did not have a home of His own. He slept on the ground most of the time. He lived with twelve men who never knew deodorant and who bathed about once a month. Yet He never complained or disputed with God.

You go on a week-long mission trip and argue over who gets the cot closest to the fan. The shower water is cold, and the bugs are everywhere. The food is thick (and it's not supposed to be). The bus breaks down in the heat of the day, and the only thing you have to drink is warm water from a canteen. The supplies for the construction site are not what you ordered, and the helpers from the church don't speak a word of English. You hit your thumb with a hammer on the first day, and the sun blisters the back of your neck. But you know this is where God led you, and you came obediently. Think you might be tempted to complain just a bit?

The aim of obedience is for us to become like Christ at every level of our lives. A mission trip is a good practice ground, but where it really matters is in our everyday, real lives. We don't do this *by ourselves*, and we don't do this *for* God. We don't say, "God, I am going to change my life, and You are going to be so pleased with how I turn out. OK, cover your eyes and I am going to surprise you."

Why doesn't God just kill us after we accept Jesus? Wouldn't it be easier if immediately afterward we just dropped dead? There would be no sin, no mistakes, no problems. The reason God leaves us here is because He chooses to deposit His Spirit in us; and over time His Spirit begins to leak His way into our minds, into our appetites, into our attitudes, into our instincts, into our lifestyles, and ultimately into our behavior. This change in us is the way God spreads His light into the darkened world. Our changed lives are a living testimony to those still in darkness.

The Spirit of God who lives inside us empowers us to live as Christ would if He were here walking in our shoes. We are being changed to think, act, and live like Christ with the people we know and in the situations we face. This is the whole point of the Christian life. The Spirit of God is empowering you and me from the inside to obediently live like Christ through every situation in life.

How do you know if you are beginning to look like Christ? You begin to have a desire to do what God wants you to do in the areas of your life where you once resisted His will. You begin to have a desire to do right. Something begins to grow inside of you that says, "I want to do what God wants me to do." You don't get this on your own; God produces it in you.

Some of the things in your life that never bothered you before now do. You come under conviction. Now the Spirit of God is working in you. Values are beginning to shift around and change your thinking, and your new thinking is beginning to change some of your behavior. All of a sudden this desire to do what God wants you to do begins to well up in you. You could go back on that miserable mission trip and actually enjoy the difficulties. This is obedience. You don't get this from religion. You don't get it apart from the work of God in you.

The ultimate aim of our obedience is to live our lives the same way Jesus lived His: dead to selfishness and alive to the life of God living in us.

Absolute Overhaul

> *...so that you will prove yourselves to be blameless and innocent, children of God above reproach...* (Philippians 2:15)

God overhauls us. He gives us a makeover from the inside out. We can't make ourselves blameless and innocent; He does that for us. It is His blamelessness and innocence placed in us that makes us above reproach.

He does this so that we will "prove" ourselves. Our makeover is not something we perform; it is something we show. The burden of proof is on God to produce these things within us, from the inside out.

The overhaul God does in us is done in three parts:

1. *He changes our hearts*. The heart is the place where our motivations and desires live. The good things and the bad things we do flow out of the heart. When God comes to live in us, He does more than just clean up our hearts; He gives us a new heart. This new heart contains the motivations and desires of God.

2. *He constructs new beliefs within us*. All of us have operated with a belief system containing lies and half-truths. Because God has placed His heart in us, He now has the foundation on which He can reconstruct our beliefs as we interact with His Word. The Scriptures reveal the lies and half-truths for what they are, and God replaces them with the truth of His Word.

3. *He creates new behavior*. Over time and with our cooperation, God's heart affects our motivations and choices. His truth changes the way we relate to life situations, and this shows up in our new behavior.

Make a decision to put the cross upright in your life. Realize that the majority of the work God does in your life is done in the vertical relationship He has with you. Over time the changes He produces deep within your character will leak out into your horizontal relationships with other people. This is where integrity and credibility originate.

If you're not in a vertical relationship with God, there is no hope for you to change by yourself. You can make some minor, temporary changes, but the real, lifelong changes God does from the inside out. The world isn't going to help you with this. The world is only concerned with surface solutions. The world says, "If you're an alcoholic, join a group and get some coffee and donuts. Have a good time. Here is a chip for being sober." The world says, "Hey, if you have trouble with smoking, put a patch on your arm." The world says, "If you are angry, just sit down and count to ten (and then load the gun)."

The world wants to put a patch over your problem. God works in the deeper levels of your life, going to the root of the problem. Whatever your invisible giant is, it is coming from some specific place inside you. Through His Spirit, God dives into the inside of your life and goes to work in the deep levels to change you.

You may not be able to feel it. It's just like growing. You didn't feel yourself growing as a child. You didn't lie in bed and say, "I'm growing. I'm getting so big that I have outgrown my bed." You do not feel yourself growing; you just end up at a certain height. Well, that's how it works spiritually. You don't always feel it. It just happens.

It happens in the context of a vertical relationship with God. As long as you are trying to change your life with the cross on its side, you are always going to struggle. You do not change yourself by changing your behavior and becoming moral. You change yourself by placing yourself in relationship, not in religion. Begin praying, "God, go to work on me. Get into the deep levels of my life and expose the things that I have not been able to see for myself. Change my desires, my attitudes, and my thoughts so that my choices fall in line with Your will for my life."

Answer Is Obvious

> *...among whom you appear as lights in the world.* (Philippians 2:15)

God doesn't produce change in us so we can become better people. We can go to a bookstore and buy tapes to learn how to become better people. He doesn't do it because we need to change our behavior and act nicely. That's cosmetic. That's all on the surface. Why does God produce change? Not for behavior, not for self-improvement. The answer is right there in the last phrase of Philippians 2:15: "*Among whom you appear as lights in the world.*" The whole incentive for character development is to make us the light of God in a world of darkness.

Galatians 5:22–23, 25 says, "*But the fruit of the Spirit is love, joy, peace, patience, kindness, goodness, faithfulness, gentleness, self-control.... If we live by the Spirit, let us also walk by the Spirit.*" When people got close to

Jesus, they saw all these things in His life. These things were the fruit of His life, and the fruit was the proof that His life was genuine. This is perhaps the most concise explanation the Bible gives us of the character of Christ.

After defining Christ's character for us, Paul tells us to take the life God places inside us and walk in it every day of our lives. God's life is supposed to be on display. We need to demonstrate it in our choices and attitudes. As the life of God overtakes our lives, we become the points God uses to reveal His presence in this world.

As we've said before, there are two characters in this world: the character of darkness and the character of light. When we put ourselves in a vertical relationship with God, we take on the character of light; and as God changes us, the difference becomes obvious. The life of God begins to shine through everything we do. Wherever we go, our lives intersect with the lives of others, and we become the light they need in the middle of their dark world.

This is the incentive and the motivation to live the life of God. Every win for God in our lives is a loss for the devil. Every time God changes us and manifests something new in us, it's a loss for darkness. When you go to do whatever your life requires of you today, remember that you do it as a light in the darkness.

Buy a cross that stands in a base. Once each day for the next week, go through the process of turning the cross on its side and then setting it right side up. As you set the cross right side up, remind yourself that true character cannot be achieved apart from a dynamic connection to the life of God living in us.

TEN

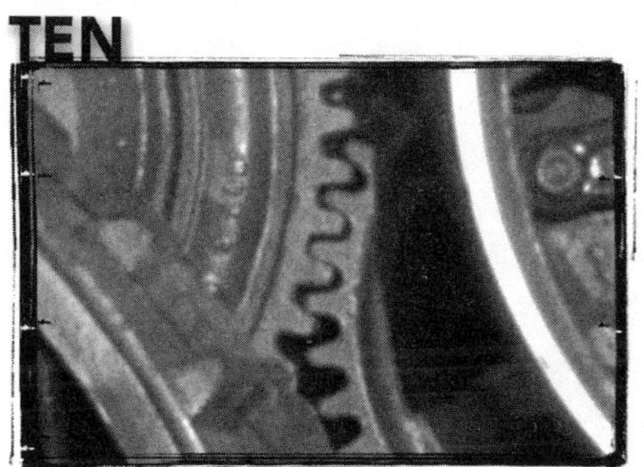

Compelling Light

THE PERSUASIVE INFLUENCE OF CHARACTER

I have traveled and spoken to people for nearly fifteen years. It's amazing to me how the battles in people's lives never seem to change. For the past fifteen years, regardless of the city I've been in, I've seen that people face the same battles, believe the same lies, and fall into the same traps.

Darkness is present in every generation. I've noticed that darkness has a mechanical character to its nature. It replicates itself like a machine stamping out the same part over and over again. It turns out the same old lies, sins, temptations, and vices. Generation after generation feels the effects of this machine's relentless production of sin.

We have lived with the effects of the machine for so long that we have grown accustomed to them. We have been deceived into thinking that what the machine produces is actual life. This false assumption draws us in, and we get caught up in the process of the machinery conforming us to its system. The goal of the machine is to get us to follow and not to think. The conformity goes so far as to get us to do what everyone else is doing, to make us look alike, believe alike, and dress alike.

The fashion mantra is, "Be different, be unique, and be cool." Then the industry invents it and tells you that you really need it. The retro movement started a fashion trend when it adopted the thrift store as its trip to the mall. Now clothes are sold that have the "vintage look." These are new clothes that look old. The jeans are frayed, faded, and scuffed. Shirts are unpressed, with tattered cuffs and collars. Purchasing this look can cost upward of a hundred dollars. It now takes a lot of money to look like you don't have any at all.

Let's say you want to be a subversive anarchist and wear all black. You might prefer to be more passive and go with the "Goth" look. (If you don't know what a "Goth" is, it's a vampire in drag.) You go to the mall and charge it. This is mass-market nonconformity. This is shopping-mall cool. It's easily attainable, and in reality it's about as edgy as Doodle Town Pipers. What we fail to realize is that it doesn't matter what our particular fashion preference is—whether it's color-blocked golf shirts, khakis with those exposed seams in the seat of the pants, or clothes with pictures and logos. (If you're going to wear clothes with pictures and logos, here's a tip: Don't mix them. In other words, don't wear a #24 Jeff Gordon hat with a #45 Kyle Petty shirt.) The fact is, all these styles have been demographically researched, funded, and produced by corporate America.

The life of God is fruit. Fruit is something that grows as opposed to something that is manufactured. It's the difference between concrete and grass. The machine of darkness takes our money, time, and energy. It robs us of understanding, knowledge, and purity. It takes everything from us. There is nothing nourishing, uplifting, or stimulating about darkness. This is why you never hear people say, "Since I started doing drugs and cheating people at work, my tithing and Scripture memorization have really improved." When was the last time you heard someone who has been sexually active say, "I'm a better person for having used people for what I can get." Victims of sexual abuse never write letters of recommendation for their attackers. Darkness is of no benefit to anyone. Darkness will cause us to lose our sense of ambition; it will steal our mission and limit our greatness.

The machine of darkness is so efficient in replicating its lies that it hasn't had to retool itself for over two generations. The boomers bought into bad sitcoms, disco, and polyester, thinking they were great ideas. Today's generation falls victim to the irony by embracing their parents' cultural idioms. They think they are being original by finding new uses for hemp, but they are really buying into the same mental trap that has enslaved millions in the patterns of dark thinking. (I once bought some cream made from hemp oil. I rubbed it on my body, and my legs wanted a brownie.)

Darkness is a machine whose gears work in unison. The movies send a message, the music makes us believe it, then fashion sells the look, and theme restaurants enshrine the lifestyle. Most notable of all the theme restaurants is the Hard Rock Café. Other knockoffs have followed: The Harley Davidson Café, the Sports Café, the WWF Café, and the Fashion Café (which I hear has no menus because models don't eat. It also has no tables...what's the point?)

These theme restaurants are decorated with memorabilia, unique guitars, a cycle seat once sat upon by someone famous, and clothes people used to dance in. These things are enshrined, and what for? Is anyone's life going to be different because of this? Each restaurant has a gift shop that sells pointless memorabilia in a place devoted to pointless memorabilia. Only darkness could have thought this up.

> *Do not participate in the unfruitful deeds of darkness, but instead even expose them.* (Ephesians 5:11)

Some time back I had lunch with a pastor friend of mine. He brought with him a young man in his early twenties who had been a minister for two years. As the meal moved on, I turned the conversation toward this young minister. "Tell us about yourself," I said. This young man had interned with a well-known pastor, and as he spoke, I realized he sounded like this pastor. He used the same phrasing, the same cadence, the same churchy language. *This is someone*, I thought to myself, *who has been manufactured.* He was a clone. He had been put into a mold and spit back out as a carbon copy of someone else.

Imitation is never pretty. You know this is true if you've ever been to an Elvis impersonators' convention. This is why we are never told to imitate the light but to become light—the genuine thing. The light born in us is born out of the character of Christ living in us. Our light comes from His light. Our experience is not someone else's experience; it's fresh. The result of our experience with Christ is uniqueness. We do not grow because of what we do; we grow because of who we are.

The question naturally follows, "How does this work for us?" We are the light of the world, and our objective is to be the light wherever we go. People hear this and say, "That may be true, but I have my career to think about. I agree with what you're saying, but I have my future to think about." Feel the tension? We live in a culture with darkened values.

One day I went to the movies with some friends, and I saw a guy I knew in the lobby. I asked him what he had been up to. He said that he had been in law school. When I asked him what law school was like, he answered, "It's rugged. I'm a believer, and that whole society is cut-throat. Everything is about competition, and people will do things just so other people in the class can't get ahead. It's completely hard-core."

"How does a believer survive in a setting like that?" I asked.

"Man, it's not easy," he said. "I almost quit last year because I couldn't take it."

That's where all of us live. We live as light in a dark world...and that's not easy. Sometimes it's so hard that we want to quit. Sometimes we wonder if we are having any positive impact at all. Sometimes we wonder if we are still *lit*.

Daniel was a young man from the Old Testament who was snatched from his hometown and forced into captivity in the foreign land of Babylon. He happened to be one of the "brightest and best" of the captured Israelites, and he was placed in a training camp designed to manufacture leaders who would be used in the service of the Babylonian king, Nebuchadnezzar. This was a society rooted in darkness, perpetuating itself through the mass production of leaders. Sameness and conformity were the orders of the day. Yet Daniel was able to authentically live out his relationship with God in such a way that people were drawn to him.

Spending time on a college campus prepares us to succeed by the world's rules. The system prepares us to do business by one set of standards. It prepares us to know the principles that it takes to get out and to get ahead. But when we give our life to Christ, we take on a new system and a new set of standards; we take on a new goal. Now we have a new tension.

The work force has its own definition of success: "Master these principles and make something great happen." But now we are beginning to understand that our lives are guided internally by a new set of principles. The principles of the *lit* life are making sense. Something deep inside us is hungry to live by these standards. There is a new tension.

We agree that it is important to live the light, yet we say, "Wait a minute! I don't want it to mess up my degree. I don't want it to mess up my job. I don't want it to mess up my future. And I sure don't want it to mess up my friendships."

How do we live our lives and still demonstrate the light and character within us in a way that is effective?

Light can be attractive or unattractive. After being in a dark room for an extended period of time, the last thing you want is to have a bright light shined in your eyes. A soft light off to the side doesn't hurt but rather invites you to step closer.

Our greatest influence doesn't happen because we look like Christians. People aren't persuaded because our haircuts are different or because we wear Christian T-shirts. Our choice of music or the fact that we get up on Sunday mornings is not persuasive to people. But there is a way that we can demonstrate the light we carry within us so that it is persuasive to people and doesn't repel them.

Daniel was able to take an uncompromising stand before people who were in authority over him. He successfully fleshed out the life of God in the middle of difficult situations. At the same time, everyone who saw him respected his life and acknowledged the power of God they saw demonstrated in his life.

The story of Daniel shows us how we can find resolution to the tension we sense when we try to live a life of character in a world with different values. Daniel helps us learn how to live in such a way that people are attracted to the light they see in us. His example gives us three principles for living as compelling light.

Rooted in Devotion

> *But Daniel made up his mind that he would not defile himself with the king's choice food or with the wine which he drank; so he sought permission from the commander of the officials that he might not defile himself.* (Daniel 1:8)

Daniel had made up his mind. He was faithful to something much greater than the society he was living in. He was motivated by something greater than his own comfort in a difficult situation. He was deeply devoted to the things of God and firmly rooted in his relationship with God. This bond between him and God was so deeply rooted that when he was dropped into the middle of darkness, he did not compromise that relationship.

When placed in a challenging situation, the first thing many of us sacrifice is our relationship with God. "Oh, Christianity is not accepted here? Well, I'll put it on the back burner to get ahead. I'll put it aside. God knows that I love Him, and I'll pick it back up when it's more convenient." Most people live this way; when challenged, we box up our spirituality and get it out of the way.

Not Daniel. He knew where he stood, and he gently stood there without being belligerent. Think about that as you work in your job or interact with society. As we move into life, we should say, "God, my deepest desire is that my life be marked internally and externally as one that belongs to You." Daniel understood the markings of God on his life. His relationship with God was the central rooting and grounding for his entire life. This devotion marked everything he did, and it was rooted in three areas: the person of God, the passion of God, and the power of God. Let's look at each one.

1. The Person of God

Daniel was rooted in his devotion to the person of God. He was in relationship with God. He loved God. He had come to know God intimately as a close friend. Daniel responded and grew in his knowledge of the person of God. Through his everyday experiences, he came to know how God thought, what God desired, and what he could expect from God.

Daniel's devotion was not to the acts of God but to the person of God. He knew that God is an all-good God; He is not the creator or the designer of evil. He knew that God is an all-time God; He always has been and always will be. He knew that God is an all-present God; He has no boundaries. He is fully present with all of His being all of the time. He knew that God is an all-knowing God; He knows everything that's knowable. He knew that God is an all-powerful God; He rules over everything in heaven and on earth. He knew that God is an all-faithful God; He doesn't change His character. And he learned all this by the time he was fifteen years old.

Daniel discovered in every circumstance of his life that he could trust God for the best solution at the best time. Daniel was so focused on the person of God that the fact that he was being held captive in a foreign land was not a major problem for him. He knew he could trust God to work everything out.

How well acquainted are you with the person of God? Do you know Him beyond what the songs tell about Him? Do you know what God thinks, or are you like most people—making guesses about the nature of God and hoping you guess right? Do you know what God desires of you in the situations you face, or do you seek the advice of friends and hope that God likes the choices you make? Do you know what you can expect from God in your struggles with life, or do you just take whatever help comes along and hope at least some of it is from Him?

Unless you are rooted in your devotion to the person of God, you will most likely fall apart when the tough times come. But when you have come to know the person of God through the everyday struggles of life, you can face the tough times knowing and trusting that the God you knew in the smaller problems is completely adequate to handle even the most difficult situation.

As a believer, you have your roots in the kingdom of light. You live in the kingdom of darkness, but you serve another king. You work in one kingdom but serve the ruler of another kingdom. You are rooted in and serve the kingdom of God ruled by the person of God. This rooting provides you with the basis for knowing the person of God like Daniel knew Him. We all come to know the person of God in the same way. Through the everyday situations we face, we learn what God thinks, what He desires, and what we can expect from Him.

Wherever you work—outside or indoors, retail or dot com—when your life moves you into a tough spot, you can face the situation rooted in the things of God. Wherever life takes you, you are forever tied to the presence and the person of God. He will never leave you or forsake you. And He is adequate for everything that touches your life.

2. The Passion of God

The heart of God defined Daniel's life. Daniel's passion was driven by the things that God was passionate about. The heartbeat of God resided in Daniel because Daniel was rooted in his personal devotion to the passion of God. The passion of God colored his perception and his thinking about everything he faced. Even at his young age, he had come to understand that holy men get close to a Holy God. His choice to pursue passion for God led him to be committed to sculpting holiness into every area of his existence. Daniel was committed to doing the will of God regardless of how it might affect his life. He was committed to the moral attributes of God's life: holiness, purity, and righteousness.

These attributes are the demonstrations of God's character. They are the things we can see. They are born from the character of God, and they are dropped into us at the same time Christ steps out of heaven and into our hearts. They are the things that are demonstrated through our lives, empowered by the godly choices we make.

For Daniel, the passion of God was more than a feeling; it defined his entire life. He clearly understood the will of God for his inner life and applied it to his heart. His will took on the life and function of God's will. This passion and commitment brought Daniel into a deep, abiding intimacy with God, and he committed himself to the same things God was committed to. He allowed the life of God to deeply imbed itself in his person, so much so that the call to and the desire for personal purity saturated every pore of his existence.

Daniel's trust that God would work everything out for good was complete. Nothing in his life was so personal or private that he would not trust God with it. He had ordered his life from the inside out, and he had predetermined how he would respond to situations. This is why, in Daniel 1:8, there was not even a question about whether or not he would eat the king's food.

When Daniel made up his mind not to eat from the royal menu, his caretakers were concerned, but they decided to let him eat the foods he chose for himself. After a time, the caretakers brought Daniel and his friends to King Nebuchadnezzar for inspection. The friends had followed Daniel's lead in not eating the food given to them. The king found that Daniel and these young men looked better and seemed wiser than any of the other men in training. They had taken their stand to live by God's standards in a tough time, and God got the credit.

Later King Nebuchadnezzar had a dream that could not be interpreted by anyone. Not one of his prophets, none of his magicians—nobody could interpret the dream for him. The dream disturbed him, and he felt it was critical to find out what it meant. So he said to his advisors, "If you can't find anyone to interpret my dream, I am going to start killing my advisory board at dawn."

A search was begun, and finally someone suggested that the advisors speak with Daniel. Daniel had interpreted other dreams; perhaps he could interpret this one for the king. Daniel was faced with an opportunity to let light shine in the darkness. He responded, "Give me some time to work it out. I need to see if God will show me what the dream means." The reason Daniel went to work at that point was not for himself; he was not out to make himself look good so he could advance his own position. He was out for the glory of God. That was Daniel's passion. What Daniel was driven by was the greater good.

As believers, we have the same drive for the greater good residing in us. That's God's own passion living inside us. As we live and work in the world of darkness, the passion of God truly motivates us from deep within. Money, power, promotions, and status are attractive and provide a lure for our self-centeredness; but we know there is something far greater, more important, and longer lasting than these temporary measures of success.

The passion of God for the greater good drives us to give Him all the glory. Daniel accomplished nothing on his own. He accomplished only what God enabled and empowered him to do. The same is true for us. God chooses to empower and enable us to accomplish His mission of taking light to the darkened world. This is the passion of God; this is what Daniel was committed to. The filter we should use for every business deal, every relationship, and every decision is the filter of giving glory to God.

3. The Power of God

Daniel was confident in the power of God. One of the things that made Daniel so attractive to the people around him was that he knew how to carry the power of God. He was confident that God would demonstrate His power in any situation that could be used to work out His purposes in Daniel's life. Daniel's confidence was not in himself; it was in the power of God.

When faced with the choice of eating food that would compromise his faith in God, Daniel stood before his caretakers with confidence and asked for a different menu. He knew that God would have to demonstrate His power if the caretakers were to allow him to have the food he asked for. Daniel's power was not in his ability to persuade the caretakers but in God's ability to change their hearts. Because of his confidence in the power of God, Daniel could face his caretakers without fear and confidently expect God's power to work things out.

When King Nebuchadnezzar had a dream, Daniel was called upon to interpret it. God gave Daniel the dream's meaning, and he stood before the king to deliver the bad news. Daniel's confidence in the power of God was so complete that he didn't fear the power of Nebuchadnezzar. He knew that God had placed him in this situation and that everything would work out for his good. The king had the power to do what he wanted with Daniel's life, but Daniel knew that God had the power to do whatever He wanted with the king's heart.

Daniel didn't develop his confidence in God's power overnight. He developed it over time as he faced more and more difficult situations. If you will begin to trust the power of God for your situations, you, too, will find yourself gaining more and more confidence in His power. As believers we have to stop being afraid that God will withhold His power from us. Take a moment and choose one situation in your life that you need to take a stand on. Pray about it and then stand. God will deliver His power in that situation. Start expecting God to demonstrate Himself.

The power of God is rooted deeply, permanently, and ever ready in the life of every believer. But you have to be rooted in your devotion to God. You can't back away. That doesn't mean you can be rude or arrogant with others. Just do as Daniel did. He simply said, "I can't eat that food." When he was confronted about interpreting the dream, he replied, "Let me pray about it." Daniel wasn't rude, arrogant, or mean. Devotion to the person of God, the passion of God, and the power of God was the most important thing in his life. People saw it, and they respected it and were drawn to it.

Refined in Decisions

Choices can sharpen character and make it more visible in our lives. Some of the important choices we make center around money, people at work, and resolving conflict wherever and whenever it arises. The choices we make in the nitty-gritty of life show the character of

God in our lives. The choices we make about the small details in life are the perfect framework for God's character to be seen in our lives.

Daniel was forced to live in a place that was not his home. The environment was hostile to his way of life, and the society accepted wickedness as the norm. But Daniel did not accept society's values or way of life as God's new and improved will for his life. No matter how dark things got where Daniel lived, God's will for him did not change. Daniel protected his commitment to developing the character of God by making the right choices. The most important decisions he made were the smaller ones that he knew would make the greatest difference in the long run.

Daniel made three decisions repeatedly. These decisions refined the character of God in his life. These three decisions act like the lens on a camera. As we apply them to our lives, they begin to refine God's character the same way a lens, when turned, brings the picture into focus.

1. Put God First in Everything

The first decision Daniel made was that God must be first in his life. The leaders came to Daniel and told him that he had to interpret the king's dream. Daniel calmly said, "You've got to give me a night to pray about it."

> *Then the mystery was revealed to Daniel in a night vision. Then Daniel blessed the God of heaven; Daniel said,…"It is He who reveals the profound and hidden things; He knows what is in the darkness, and the light dwells with Him. To You, O God of my fathers, I give thanks and praise, for You have given me wisdom and power; even now You have made known to me what we requested of You."* (Daniel 2:19–20, 22–23)

Daniel recognized that by himself he couldn't interpret his own dreams, much less the king's dreams. He had interpreted other dreams for his caretakers, but he knew that even those interpretations came from God. Daniel put God first. He went to God in prayer. He requested some time to pray rather than launching out in his own strength to interpret the dream for the king. As a result, God answered Daniel's prayer. He told Daniel what the dream meant.

How much more practical could this be? We should put God first in all that we do: projects, finances, and relationships. The consequences of most of our choices in these areas are not a matter of life and death, like they were for Daniel. If Daniel hadn't come up with the dream's meaning, not only could he have lost his life, but many other people would have died too.

Where does God need to be put first in your life? Choosing to put God first is the first step in the refining of character. It focuses our attention on the Author and Finisher of character. It helps us gain insight and confidence to face any situation with the knowledge that God will work it out for our good.

2. Do Nothing without God's Permission

The second decision Daniel made was to do nothing without God's permission.

> *So Daniel went in and requested of the king that he would give him time, in order that he might declare the interpretation to the king. Then Daniel went to his house and informed his friends...about the matter, so that they might request compassion from the God of heaven concerning this mystery, so that Daniel and his friends would not be destroyed with the rest of the wise men of Babylon.* (Daniel 2:16–18)

Daniel didn't just pray by himself; he went to his friends and asked them to pray with him. Daniel had his sights set on gaining permission from God to give the king what he needed. He asked his friends to pray for him so that he would know that he was in the will of God. They joined him in prayer, asking God for the interpretation of the dream. They also gave Daniel the encouragement and counsel he needed to remain faithful to his commitment to operate only out of the permission of God.

For us, this means we do *nothing* without God's permission. We move the permission of God to the forefront of every decision we have to make. We don't move into relationships without permission from God. We don't move into a business deal unless we have permission from God to do it. We don't move into some new venture, opportunity, or event unless we know we have permission from God.

The American way of doing things is to decide what you want to do and then ask God to bless it. That is what most people do. "Here is what I'm going to do, God. Here's my course schedule. Here's the job I'm going to take. Here is what I'm going to buy. Now You bless me and make it happen." In reality it should be the other way around. We should be saying, "God, I won't do it if You don't want me to do it." We should be telling others, "Unless I know that I have permission and peace from God, you can count me out."

We understand what God gives us permission to do as we consistently read God's Word, as we seek godly council, and as we come to a sense of peace in our hearts. When these three things line up, we know we have permission, and we can be confident of the blessing of God.

3. Live God's Will, Whatever the Cost

The third decision Daniel made was to live God's will regardless of the personal cost. After God revealed to him what the dream meant, Daniel went to King Nebuchadnezzar and told him, "You're going down, and your kingdom is going to fall." Daniel told him that the kingdom of God was going to rise and take over all earthly kingdoms. He said, "All the kingdoms that are coming behind you are going to fall. But there is one coming that is the one great kingdom, and it will never fall."

> *In the days of those kings the God of heaven will set up a kingdom which will never be destroyed, and that kingdom will not be left for another people; it will crush and put an end to all these kingdoms, but it will itself endure forever.* (Daniel 2:44)

Daniel risked his life and everything he had to stand in front of the most powerful man in the land and deliver the truth. Daniel had no clue how the king would react. He walked into that meeting facing possible death. He knew that if Nebuchadnezzar chose to, he could kill the one who interpreted the dream. Daniel knew the risk he faced from this earthly king. But he knew that the greater risk was to fail in his obedience to his first love, His God and Father.

A friend of mine started a dot-com company a few years ago. It grew and attracted the attention of some businesspeople who wanted to purchase it. The Web site is unabashedly Christian. The businesspeople contacted my friend and offered him a more-than-fair amount to purchase the site. They also offered him the job of CEO as part of the deal. The only catch was that Jesus would have to be completely removed from the Web site. My friend walked away from the negotiation table without selling the company. He could have made millions, but he chose to keep Jesus public on his site. A few days later he received a call from the same people, this time saying that they respected his convictions. They made the same offer but allowed Jesus to remain public on the site. By the way, my friend is now a very wealthy CEO.

There will be times when the cost of your obedience to God will be the risk of losing something you love. Living God's will could cost you a job, a relationship, money, or the respect of others. At those times you must choose, like Daniel, to obey regardless of the cost.

Results in Demonstration

After Daniel delivered the interpretation, the king bowed down to Daniel and Daniel's God. This wicked king was able to see the kingdom of light in the life of someone he had brought in as a servant-in-training!

> *Then King Nebuchadnezzar fell on his face and did homage to Daniel.... The king answered Daniel and said, "Surely your God is a God of gods and a Lord of kings and a revealer of mysteries."* (Daniel 2:46–47)

Isn't this what we want for our country? Isn't this what we hope will happen in every corporation, company, and retail store? Isn't this what we desire for every school, family, and church? We want to live in such a way that the people trapped in darkness are attracted to the light of God in us, not repelled by it. We long for people to say, "What you have is real. You serve the living and true God!"

When character properly demonstrates the light, people see it and are drawn to it. There are three ways character results in a proper demonstration of light.

1. Personal Victory

After the king confessed that Daniel served the one true God, Daniel was appointed to be the ruler over the entire province. God brought Daniel his success. Instead of thinking that we have to either live for God *or* be successful, we need to realize that our character is rooted in our devotion to God and refined as we make proper decisions. Proper decisions result in the demonstration of the full character of God in our lives. Then God makes sure we experience personal victory. Daniel was promoted, and everyone knew why. It was completely a God thing. Isn't that our greatest hope? That people would look at us and say, "I see. It's God in you. I get it"?

Ultimately, blessing and promotion come from God. When we do God's things in God's way, blessing and promotion will follow. We don't have to compromise our relationship with God or violate our character in order to experience personal success.

2. World Impact

Daniel served as ruler through the Babylonian reign, the Persian reign, and the Medes reign. Ultimately he served Cyrus, the king who signed the papers to finally free the Israelites from bondage. He became an advisor to these four major, dominant regimes. And he served until he was nearly eighty years old! He had incredible access to the most powerful men in the land, and he didn't have to compromise his beliefs and values to get there. He didn't have to be a religious jerk to get there either. Who wouldn't like to have an eighty-year-long life of success, do well, get promoted, and see their greatest dreams come true? Daniel was a man who did it all. His life is our example for changing our world.

3. Provoking Challenge

Daniel was a man who lived life right. He passionately faced the challenges of life head-on, knowing who he was in God. The example of his life compelled others to live for God and challenges us to live as he did. When we take on the character of Christ, the rules for our lives change. While all of our friends are cutting corners and doing things that are unethical, we live by a different standard. As believers, the world's rules of success won't work for us.

Your promotion is going to come through Somebody Else, not your boss. You are in God's hands. He knows where you are and what you face every day. He knows that you are facing some of the toughest issues you have ever confronted. No matter what you face, no matter how weary you feel, no matter how dark things look, God will give you favor with the people you work with, and the best promotion for you is yet to come.

The challenge for us is to live our lives in such a way that we become the light of the world. The challenge is to live in such a way that this world sees the light and is drawn to it. Living as light is no little thing. We must never forget the impact that Daniel's choices had on nations and governments. Our choices also have the potential to impact lives around the world.

You have an opportunity to demonstrate the character of God through following the example of Daniel. Commit yourself to the heart of God. Make choices that strengthen the character of God within you. Your life can be a compelling light that draws many people one step closer to the kingdom of Christ if you'll just go for it.

Daniel and his friends were rooted in their devotion to God and went so far as to demonstrate that devotion by the things they allowed to touch—or not touch—their lives. Every day this week choose something, such as a food item or a form of entertainment, that you will do without for the day. As you do without this item, let this remind you that everything touching your life should reinforce the character of Christ in you.

ELEVEN

Right Light

IT MUST BE RIGHT TO BE LIGHT

Sports—the national pastime. A celebration of champions. The early days of sports were a simpler time. The story was always easy to follow. A young man works hard, plays fair for the love of the game, becomes a hero in the eyes of the fans, and in turn gives his affection back to the fans and rides off into the sunset.

These days the story is slightly different. A young man drops out of school for a hefty signing bonus, lives excessively in a self-indulgent fog, does drugs, gets in vicious brawls, spits at the fans, beats women, becomes a felon, goes through tedious court proceedings, is exonerated because of who he is, and drives recklessly into the sunset in his brand-new Porsche.

All the blue blocker sunglasses you can find will not screen out what the fans can see from the stands. Players are disloyal, spoiled, ill-mannered parolees. If it weren't for sports, kids wouldn't know what organized crime looks like. Coaches are raving madmen, and gasoline is still cheaper than the stadium hot dogs.

Bad sportsmanship is now the norm. Winning with class and dignity and losing heroically are about as relevant as a Beta video player. Winning is not enough. Now the opponent has to be humiliated. After every block or touchdown, a player dances, makes mocking moves, and points a finger in the loser's face. This idea of "winning at all costs," or "the ends justify the means," has removed most of the fun from watching the game. The essence of the game has moved from enjoying the game to making the game profitable.

We, the fans, have given these guys a status they don't deserve. At the same time the O. J. trial was taking place, there was another man being tried for the same crime. His trial was over in three weeks, and no one ever heard of it. Why do we give these guys respect? We throw out the rules of right and wrong just because they are good at P.E. What's right and what's wrong should be the same for all of us. Whether we live in a lavish mansion or a lean-to, the rules should be the same.

(Now, I'm not busting on all athletes. I can't make the same statements about women athletes. Assault, murder, ear biting, date rape—the women don't do these things. If you were to put all the women athletes together, they would still have a shorter rap sheet than the Dallas Cowboys.)

I can hear the screams from the sidelines. Yes, there are Christian athletes who have remained sexually and morally pure. This once again proves my point. We've made these guys into heroes for doing what they're supposed to do. Isn't every Christian supposed to be morally and sexually pure? This is how rare right is. When someone does something right, it's lauded as extraordinary.

I know this is harsh, but what is happening in sports is a microcosm of what's going on in America. From politics to business to personal life, we've lost the ability to know what is right and to do it.

I don't watch many sports on TV, but I do watch some when I happen to be at home. My mom loves sports. We were watching a football game one Sunday afternoon and saw a pass play in which the receiver dropped the ball. It was almost a reception, but the receiver juggled the ball as he fell to the ground. The referee was out of position and couldn't see whether he had actually caught it or not. The player rolled over the ball, grabbed it, and stood up celebrating as if he had made a miraculous catch. The referee was fooled, the player ran back to the huddle, and his team hurried the next play before anyone had time to review the tape.

Those of us watching from home had the benefit of the replay. We clearly saw what the referee missed. The ball hit the ground and bounced back into the receiver's hands. The commentators ran the tape back and forth several times and then said, "That kid played some heads-up football!" What they really meant was, "That kid is a great liar, but he helped his team get the first down. Way to go!"

I was blown away by the commentators' words, but they paint a clear picture of America's character dilemma. We cry out for the character of our country to be improved. But while we deplore overt criminal activity, we endorse winning at all costs. When push comes to shove, we'll do just about anything to be on the winning side.

If the player had gone to the referee and said, "I'm sorry, man, but your call is wrong—I didn't catch that ball," he probably would have been yelled at by the coach, his teammates, and the fans. They would have said he was not a team player. I guess the good team player lies to the referee. I guess the real ethics behind the game reward the cheaters rather than those who play by the rules.

It seems that in football and in life, Americans have lost the ability to distinguish right from wrong. If we are going to regain that ability, we must know if the choices we are making are the right ones. For some the right choices are the legal choices. As long as it's legal, it's OK. For many the criterion for right choices is what is socially acceptable. As long as enough people think it's OK, then it's OK. That leaves us with the people who don't care if it's legal or popular; they base their choices simply on their own personal preferences or what they think they can get away with.

Whether or not they put it into these words, many people would say this about the player who deceived the referee: "We can't pass judgment on him because we really don't know the rules for following the rules." America has accepted a floating definition of right. "Just because someone says something is right or wrong doesn't make it so for me." "Just because there is a rule to follow doesn't mean that it's always the right thing for me to do." When the rules are too inconvenient or uncomfortable, we simply change the rules for following the rules.

The reality is, Christians have bought into this lie too. We have chosen the world's definition of "right." We have adopted the world's rules for following the rules. We have tolerated the world's character for so long that it has become our own. But God has absolutes about what is right and wrong. And He has given believers four ways to know if the choices we make are pleasing to Him and consistent with His character. In God's mind, it must be light to be right.

We find these four principles in the story of David from 1 Samuel 24. David was being pursued by Saul, the king of Israel, because Saul was jealous of David's popularity and God's obvious favor upon his life. David and his men found themselves hiding in a desert cave, with Saul and his army drawing close. This real-life interaction between David, his men, and Saul clearly illustrates how David chose between right and wrong.

Availability Is No Reason

> *Now when Saul returned from pursuing the Philistines, he was told, saying, "Behold, David is in the wilderness of Engedi." Then Saul took three thousand chosen men from all Israel and went to seek David and his men in front of the Rocks of the Wild Goats. He came to the sheepfolds on the way, where there was a cave; and Saul went in to relieve himself. Now David and his men were sitting in the inner recesses of the cave. The men of David said to him, "Behold, this is the day of which the LORD said to you, 'Behold; I am about to give your enemy into your hand, and you shall do to him as it seems good to you.'" Then David arose and cut off the edge of Saul's robe secretly.* (1 Samuel 24:1–4)

Saul entered the cave, not realizing that David and his men were hiding inside just a few yards away. One of David's men encouraged him, "Kill Saul, and our days of running will be over." David had an opportunity to kill the man who was trying to kill him. He had an opportunity to prove himself the hero in the eyes of his men. He had the opportunity, but he passed on it because it was wrong. Just because we have the opportunity to do something doesn't make it right.

I have had many opportunities to snow ski while speaking at retreats. I love the mountains; the cold, crisp air; and the fireplaces. But I know my ability to break bones and pull tendons. Skiing is not right for me. Give me the opportunity, and I'll pass every time.

Women, just because you have the opportunity to date a guy doesn't mean you should. Sure, he's handsome and has lots of money. Sure, he would look good on your dating resume. Sure, it would raise your net worth in the popularity polls. Does it really matter that he's the son of Satan and his eyes glow without the help of a black light? He's standing in front of you asking you out. You have the opportunity, but is it right? You're available, but is that a good enough reason to take the date?

I grew up with a guy, and we played in a band together. He is now married, and I'm still close with him and his wife. The only thing is, he now has three screaming kids. I don't bond well with kids. They all look like little drunk people to me. I do like the fact that they're usually small in stature, which makes them useful when cleaning those really hard-to-reach places. And I have to admit that every time I'm lying on the couch and realize I've left the remote on the TV, I wish I had a kid who could go get it for me. (I really love my life.) The truth is, I don't know what to say to kids. I say "hello," and that's it. I'm done. I never learned kid-speak, and for that matter, I don't want to. It's a foreign language to me—and I'd like to keep it that way.

My friend's wife came to hear me speak one time, and she brought her three kids with her. After the crowd had cleared out, she brought the kids over to me. I greeted her, and the kids just stared at me like they were watching my lips turn blue or something. I rolled my eyes, smiled, and asked her, "So, how's everything?" What she told me hit me so hard that I just stared back. "Not very good," she said. "I'm getting ready to leave him. I just can't take it anymore."

I asked her if my friend knew what she was thinking and feeling. "No, he doesn't know," she said. "I'm taking the kids and going back home so my family can help me watch them. I just can't do this anymore."

I knew she was hurting. These were my friends. I didn't think about what to say; it just came out. "Don't you dare!" I told her. She flinched and so did I, but I didn't stop. "So help me, if you leave him, I will track you down and physically drag you back home. That's a promise!"

She knows me well enough to know that I don't make vain promises. I would have tracked her down. I would have gotten help with the dragging home part, but I would have tracked her down.

"But I could go back home to my family," she said. "If I leave him I'll be much happier than I am now."

I had calmed down a bit by that point, so I told her, "Just because you have the opportunity to take the kids and go home, just because your parents will help, just because you checked this out with some of your friends who support your decision—that doesn't make it right."

David understood all this. He could have chosen to kill Saul. Saul was available for the killing, but that didn't make it right. Availability is no reason.

Agreement Is No Rationale

> *The men of David said to him, "Behold, this is the day...." It came about afterward that David's conscience bothered him because he had cut off the edge of Saul's robe. So he said to his men, "Far be it from me because of the LORD that I should do this thing to my lord, the LORD'S anointed."* (1 Samuel 24:4–6)

Just because everyone says we should do something doesn't make it acceptable. All of David's men agreed, "This is it! You should kill Saul. There won't be another opportunity like this. Just kill him and we'll all go home." Any of us can find a friend to confirm what our scheming hearts approve of. And if one of our friends won't confirm it, we can always make a new friend who will.

Just because everyone says it's OK doesn't make it OK. The majority is always wrong. It was the majority that killed Jesus. Man left to himself and the majority will end up destroying himself. "Everyone says I should do it. Everyone says it's OK." But agreement is no rationale.

Our whole country functions on the vote. Everything is up for a vote. Political careers are won and lost on a vote. When there isn't an election going on, someone is taking a survey asking our opinions. Advertisers send us forms to fill out so they can learn our shopping preferences. And if that's not enough, now interactive TV allows us to vote from the comfort of our easy chairs.

Daytime TV talk shows are all about the vote; they're all about consensus. They bring out some guy with an alternative lifestyle who likes to stick knives in his head. The announcer says, "Today, from St. Louis, we have Ed, who likes to stick knives into his head." The entire audience—everyone to a person—grimaces at the sight of the knives sticking out of Ed's head. But it isn't long before someone takes the mike and says, "Well, I think he should have the right to do it. In fact, I think someone should form a coalition for people who stick knives in their heads." The talk show host turns to the audience and asks, "What does everyone think?" The room erupts with approval. "Oh, we approve of it. You should do that." After the noise dies down, some poor soul in the crowd raises his hand. The host walks over and sticks the microphone in his face, and the person says, "You know, if you stick knives in your head, you are going to have a big, bleeding wound." Against such reckless insensitivity the crowd screams, "Boo! Sit down!"

The whole point of the show is to build a case that everyone can agree with. The host winds up the show saying something like, "This country affords everyone the freedom of self-expression. Ed has chosen to express himself in this way, and most of our audience agrees that Ed should be allowed to express himself as he sees fit. When you meet the 'Ed' in your neighborhood, I hope you will encourage him to do as he pleases. After all, people have the right to do what they want to do."

There's a difference between the *rights* that we have and what's *right*. Remember, it has to be light to be right.

In a corporate setting, one of the commonly accepted practices is to close a deal over drinks. This may be the norm for your company, and many of your clients may expect it. I know what you're thinking. The Bible never says, "Don't drink." It never explicitly says that drinking is wrong. But character is an issue of ownership. Who owns you, you or the life of God living in you? If your answer is the life of God in you, then others may drink, but does that make it right for you? It must be light to be right.

Whether we understand it or not, Christians live under a higher authority than the crowd. Just because everyone says it's right doesn't make it so. Agreement is no rationale. If we are going to personally know something is right, we have to have a word from God. I'm not talking about a cryptic message revealed in a freak refrigerator fire that leaves your fridge untouched but scrawls the words of a revelation on your ceiling in smoke stains. It's not nearly that complicated. We must know that God approves of what we do. Here are some ways we can know if something is God's will.

Read Scripture

As we start reading the Bible from the front of the book all the way through to the end of that book, the Spirit of God points out verses to us—they kind of pop out. They touch us in the heart. It's almost as if God is speaking directly to us through the pages of the Bible. There are certain phrases that have a specific meaning to us. As we read, God deals with the subjects that are on our minds through the Scripture.

Whatever you are wondering about, talk with God about it. Then get into His Word. Don't expect the answer the first time you read...but then again, don't limit God. Make the reading of the Bible a daily priority in your schedule.

This is more than reading a little verse off a calendar and saying, "Oh, now I'll have a good day." It's more than reading about someone who lost his bike, prayed, and found it again. A devotional magazine isn't the Bible. You have to sit down and ask God, "Speak to me through Your Word. Show me who You are and what You approve of!"

By the way, I've found it very helpful to have something to write on when I'm reading the Bible. God never ceases to amaze me with the things He speaks to me through the time I read His Word.

The courts are jammed-packed with frivolous lawsuits. Take the lady who spilled hot coffee on herself as she pulled away from the McDonald's drive-through. She sued and got three million dollars. Sure, she has the right to sue, but is it right? God's Word says in Micah 6:11, *"Can I justify wicked scales and a bag of deceptive weights?"* It must be light to be right.

"Everyone should do his own thing as long as he doesn't hurt anyone" is a phrase that has been used more times than a port-a-john at a Promise Keepers conference. Doing your own thing and not hurting anyone are not always compatible. In his book *Landscape of the Soul*, Douglas V. Porpora says the problem with a morality that is "largely procedural is that it does not identify any moral purpose we ought to fulfill with our lives."[1] No matter how right your own thing may seem, it must be light to be right.

Pay Attention to Your Desires

God places His desires in our hearts. (Read about it in Romans 8.) He doesn't ask us to do things we hate. A certain thing may not be one of our favorite choices at the moment, but over time, if it is something God wants us to do, He will place the proper desire in our hearts.

I don't fight God about speaking to groups of people every night. I love what I do. I have a desire to do it. (You're probably saying, "And who wouldn't?") But you know, being on the road looks more glamorous than it is. Most of the time, I have my office ship boxes of clothes for me to wear for the next three weeks. And then I return the favor—I ship back my dirty clothes. Come to think of it, life on the road is fairly glamorous. I haven't done laundry in years.

I've been on the road for the last eleven years, and I absolutely love it. When I was sixteen, that desire was placed inside of me. Over time, as I read the Scripture, God confirmed that what I desired was what He desired for me.

These first two ingredients go together: read the Bible and pay attention to your desires. What do you have an affinity for? If you have two or three things that you really enjoy, which do you really want to do? If you are leaning more in one direction than another, you need to ask God to confirm it. Is that your desire or His? As you read the Bible, pray, "Help me to know that I have your approval to do this."

Can you imagine how different our dating lives would be if we did this? What if we prayed about the date before we asked the person to go out? What if we asked God what He thought before we accepted the date? "Listen, God, I don't want to do this unless it's right. Just because this person is available is no rationale. Just because all my friends are saying I should go out is no reason for me to do it." Imagine how different our lives would be if we said, "God, help me to know that I'm hanging out with the right people, that I'm going out with the right people, that I'm joining myself emotionally to the people You approve of." Christianity is about what we do in the details of our lives. The only way we find out what's right, the only way we find out God's will, is through reading Scripture and paying attention to our desires.

Seek Godly Counsel

We need to have some godly people in our lives who have experienced more of the God life than we have. They need to have walked with God longer than we have and understand the things of God in ways we don't. We need people in our lives to whom we can go and ask, "What do you think?"

The five men in my life who see my deepest motives know me inside and out—the good, the bad, and the ugly. I have made a commitment to be completely open and honest with them. They can ask me any question, and I will answer it honestly—no matter how badly it might make me look. When I need advice, I turn to them. They confirm the things that I must do and keep me away from things that I should not do.

Christianity is not a solo sport. You're supposed to have people in your life who can give you godly counsel. That's the value of being part of a church. In spite of what people may tell you, regardless of how you feel about being this open and vulnerable with anyone, you need to make sure that you are doing what is right and pleasing to God. We often play with foolish and petty toys, missing out on God's best, because we accept what is easily available and what the crowd cheers us toward.

Authority Must Not Be Refused

> *David persuaded his men with these words and did not allow them to rise up against Saul. And Saul arose, left the cave, and went on his way. Now afterward David arose and went out of the cave and called after Saul, saying, "My lord the king!" And when Saul looked behind him, David bowed with his face to the ground and prostrated himself.*
>
> *David said to Saul, "Why do you listen to the words of men, saying, 'Behold, David seeks to harm you'? Behold, this day your eyes have seen that the LORD had given you today into my hand in the cave, and some said to kill you...and I said, 'I will not stretch out my hand against my lord, for he is the LORD'S anointed.' Now, my father, see! Indeed, see the edge of your robe in my hand! For in that I cut off the edge of your robe and did not kill you, know and perceive that there is no evil or rebellion in my hands, and I have not sinned against you, though you are lying in wait for my life to take it.... As the proverb of the ancients says, 'Out of the wicked comes forth wickedness'; but my hand shall not be against you."* (1 Samuel 24:7–11, 13)

Saul had made some tremendous mistakes in judgment. He had listened to unrighteous counsel and missed God's plan for the kingdom. He had listened to the crowd cheering approval for David and chose jealousy and anger over strong leadership. By chasing David, he had shown everyone just what a weak and unfit king he was.

Saul had been anointed the first king of Israel. God had handpicked him for the position. His authority over the land was rooted in the authority of God, but somewhere along the way, Saul forgot that. The power went to his head, and he became so caught up in his own importance that he thought he needed to protect his position. He took the advice of his counselors and friends and tried to kill David.

David had already been anointed the next king of Israel. God had also handpicked him for the position. His authority over the land was rooted in the same place as Saul's, but David was not yet enthroned; he was in hiding. The difference between the two men was that David was committed to doing the right thing. David had been taught not to raise his hand against God's anointed. He trusted God's hand rather than his own. He waited on God to produce what had been promised. To do the right thing in the wrong way is still wrong.

I heard a story about a man who was an excellent homebuilder. He had worked for a very wealthy man for many years, building hundreds of homes in several subdivisions throughout a particular city. The man never made a great deal of money and felt that his boss never really paid him what he was worth. He built the homes he was instructed to build, but his resentment eventually turned to bitterness. One day, after almost thirty years of working for the wealthy man, he decided to quit. When he turned in his notice, the wealthy man was surprised but accepted it with one condition. "You must build me one more house," the wealthy man said. "It will be quite an elaborate house and will take you several months to complete. While you are building the house, I will double your pay, and if you complete it before the specified date, I will give you a bonus."

The homebuilder reluctantly agreed and set about the task of building the last house. Weeks went by, and the project made quick progress. The homebuilder sped up the process by cutting corners and using inferior materials that were in stock rather than the special-order materials the wealthy man had requested. The home was built in record time and looked great. But underneath the attractive facade, the structure was completely inferior.

The homebuilder reported to the wealthy man that the home was completed before the deadline and said that he would like to collect his last check and the bonus he was promised. The wealthy man cut the check and handed the man his bonus: the keys to the house he had just built. "You have been a faithful worker for many years, and I am grateful for all you have done for me and my company. As a way of saying thank you, I want you to have this house for your retirement home."

Doing the right thing in the wrong way is still wrong! Colossians 3:23 says, "*Whatever you do, do your work heartily, as for the Lord rather than for men.*"

Even though David was an innocent man being hunted, it was still wrong for him to kill Saul. His life was on the line, but he knew that he was not permitted by God to kill the Lord's anointed.

It Always Brings Results

> *[Saul] said to David, "You are more righteous than I; for you have dealt well with me, while I have dealt wickedly with you.... Now, behold, I know that you will surely be king, and that the kingdom of Israel will be established in your hand."* (1 Samuel 24:17, 20)

David passed up the opportunity to kill the man who was chasing him. In doing so, he was able to fulfill what he was designed by God to do. When you and I get into a sticky situation, we think it may be our only opportunity to act, so we force the issue. We do what feels right, or what our friends tell us is right, instead of finding out what God says is right. We forget that it is God who does the work, not us.

God had chosen David to be king, and David trusted in the Lord's power to accomplish what was promised. It didn't matter how things looked on the surface; God would produce the end results in His time and in His way. Doing things God's way always brings results. In fact, it brings immediate results.

We can experience the same results David experienced. As soon as David did what was right, he experienced two things.

1. There Was Peace in His Life

Why are we so surprised when we feel bad after doing the wrong thing? Sorrow is the natural consequence of sin—not an unexpected result. Choosing to do the wrong thing will always result in a lack of peace. David turned away from sin, did the right thing, and the immediate result was peace.

I received an e-mail from a young man who had entered the ministry several years before and was regularly attending one of my Bible studies for the teaching and fellowship. "I found myself *doing* Christianity but had no real dependence on God," he wrote. "I taught myself how to sin and still look holy." His choices resulted in the loss of his ministry. He returned home to work in his father's construction business.

He related the story to me: "I spent about four months working in the heat of the day, and that left me with many hours to think about my life and my priorities. During those long, hot months I listened to your talks on character and the price of genuine character. I made the commitment to pay the price, and man, was it expensive! But I wouldn't trade the peace and fulfillment I now have in my life for anything I've given up."

2. He Became the King

Obedience always brings positive results. Ultimately David became king in place of Saul, just as God had promised. It's unrealistic to think that our obedience today will result in a kingship; but the plans and results God has for each of us are just as important as they were for David. Obedience solidifies these results in our lives.

It pays to make sure you're doing the right thing. You don't have to compromise to get what you want. You don't have to compromise your time, your money, or your body in order to be happy. Compromise will only bring sorrow. Want proof? Just look at Saul's life!

For the believer whose life is in Christ, the truth of this chapter should begin to make sense. The motivation for doing the right thing is the continued development of character in our lives. This doesn't mean that we won't be tempted to listen to what our friends tell us is the right thing to do. It does mean that we have the ability to look beyond the immediate to the eternal. Because God lives in us, we have the ability to think differently, choose differently, and expect much different results.

Christopher was fifteen years old when he was shot while playing basketball a few blocks away from a hospital in Chicago. A couple of his friends helped Christopher make his way to the hospital; but thirty feet outside the hospital's doors, he collapsed, unable to go any further. Afraid of injuring him further, his friends ran into the emergency room and pleaded with the medical staff to come outside and help. But the staff refused to get involved. Hospital policy prohibited them from leaving the hospital out of concern for the legal liability should they neglect patients already inside. Instead, the staff placed a 911 call while Christopher lay bleeding on the sidewalk thirty feet away. It was nearly twenty-five minutes before a police sergeant commandeered a hospital wheelchair and brought Christopher into the emergency room. The fifteen-year-old boy died a few moments later.

Thirty feet inside the hospital or thirty feet outside the hospital makes little difference. There were people in both places who needed more attention paid to them than to the hospital rule that prohibited the staff from helping anyone outside the door. The hospital staff probably experienced many emotions in the few minutes they were faced with this dilemma. They may have even grieved over Christopher and the fact that "their hands were tied." We don't know what they felt, but what we do know is that they chose the expedient over the right.

To be people of God, we can't do the expedient thing. We must do the right thing. And the right thing is always God's will. Before you do anything based on emotions or circumstances or what someone tells you to do, seek the Lord God Almighty. You must answer this question: Will your decisions flow out of your relationship with Christ? If not, you will most likely make the wrong decision. Never forget: It must be light to be right.

Consider your lifestyle. In what ways are you broadcasting values, principles, or desires that are not in line with your true character? Identify one of these areas and make it right.

TWELVE

Amplify Light

ANSWER YOUR CRITICS WITH RESULTS

Several years ago I spoke on a tour that lasted a number of months. I was in many different churches but traveled with the same group of people. I had the same band and the same production staff the whole time. When the tour started, I didn't know any of these guys. The tour coordinators just called me up and asked if I wanted to be their speaker. Well, that's what I do for a living—so I signed on, not really knowing what I was getting into.

At each meeting, part of the regular program called for all the youth to remain in the meeting hall while the youth pastors and adult sponsors went to another room. There, they would be given information about various products and upcoming events. For the first two weeks, I never went back to this room, but at one point in the third week, I decided to drop in just to say "hi" and see what went on.

When I got back to the room, I saw a guy setting up donuts and putting out gallons of orange juice on long tables. I had seen this person before but knew him only by face. I walked over and said, "Well, three weeks down. So far so good. What do you think?"

"Well," he said, "I think everybody liked the speaker we had last year a whole lot better than they like you."

Without thinking I responded, "Bro, you are the donut guy. Look at you. You are back here setting out donuts and pouring juice. What a job!" I regretted the words as soon as they came out of my mouth, but I just couldn't believe what he'd said. I couldn't help thinking to myself, *What a jerky thing to say to somebody!*

It turned out that this scene was just the trailer for the rest of a really bad film in which I played a strong supporting role. For the next several weeks, every time I saw the donut guy, he had something negative to say to me—something negative about my talks, something negative about what happened in the program. I knew every time I got on the plane with the team, that guy was going to be there. I had to learn how to deal with him, and that struggle is where the principles in this chapter come from.

There's a whole world of pastry critics out there (and I don't mean pastry tasters). You can spot them anywhere. Like pastries, these critics come in a wide variety.

There are the "Honey Buns." These are the ones who always appear to be sweet and say they're your best friend but end up backhanding you with unsweetened criticism.

The "Bama Pies" are the ones who welcome you with a smile but silently say, "He's different...let's get him." Every criticism is shrouded in some reference to football, like (spoken in a southern accent), "We're gonna roll-tide you right out 'a here, boy!"

The "Zingers" always come in threes or fours. These are critics packaged to look like committees. They never face you alone but feed off each other's feelings. They may claim to be telling you something "for your own good," but it's easy to see that this icing is anything but sweet.

The "Twinkies" are everywhere. No matter where you go, you'll find them. Their critical spirits have the shelf life of the real sponge cake; they never go away. They are the ones who would have something negative to say about the second coming of Christ: "The horns are too loud!" "You came in the middle of the night!" "The dead got to go first!"

All of these critics pale in comparison to the king: "Ding Dong." He is the head of all critics. He is the guy who knows how to push all the right buttons in our lives. Sometimes just the sight of King Ding Dong is enough to set us off.

Every one of us is going to have "donut guys" in our lives. Some of them we are going to date, some of them we are going to work for, and some of them we are going to live with. We have to know how to maintain our character. How do we handle the jerks? How do we respond to the pastry critics? How do we live out the character of God when faced with these kinds of people?

Sometimes the attack you get will be unintentional, and other times it will be deliberate. Sometimes it will be major, and other times it will be minor. It doesn't matter how the attack comes; just know that it will come. Your character *will* be attacked.

Principles of the Attack

As we saw in chapter 10, Daniel was a man of compelling character. When people came around him, they were drawn to him because of his character. When we take on the light of God, we want to express it in a way that ensures that people are drawn to it and not repelled by it. Critical, cynical, mean-spirited Christians do the kingdom of God more harm than good. For many people, their only experience with God is an encounter with some mean-spirited Christian shooting off Scripture bullets that question their character and motivations.

There will be times when our character is tested. The Bible always links character and testing. Testing, trials, and tribulations can refine character in us, as the Scripture says: "*knowing that tribulation brings about perseverance; and perseverance, proven character*" (Romans 5:3–4).

Character is worthless if it's not applied in life. If all we do is hold on to character and say, "I have God living in me, and it doesn't matter about everyone else," other people are left out in the darkness with little hope of finding the light. It doesn't do us any good to hold on to character and claim it for ourselves while shunning others. Character kept to ourselves is not character at all. The intent of character is to be lived out. And character is applied and tested the most when we come under attack. It is then that we really come face to face with the challenge of living out what we say we believe.

There are some important things that you must understand when your character is attacked.

Caused by Someone You Know

> *It seemed good to Darius to appoint 120 satraps over the kingdom, that they would be in charge of the whole kingdom, and over them three commissioners (of whom Daniel was one).* (Daniel 6:1–2)

Daniel had just emerged from a great prophetic situation, described in Daniel 5, in which the finger of God appeared at one of King Belshazzar's parties and wrote a message on the wall. Everyone wondered, "What does it mean? Does anybody have a decoder ring?" Daniel stepped forward and said, "You don't need a decoder ring. I can tell you what it means." Daniel told Belshazzar what the message said, and the king was killed. As a result, a new king, Darius, came to power, and Daniel walked out of that situation and into a promotion. Daniel was one of three men put in charge of the 120 satraps (the men given responsibility for the administration of the country).

Daniel's work partners—the other commissioners and the satraps—were the ones that ended up attacking him. When an attack comes against your character, most of the time it will not come from a stranger; it will be caused by someone you know. The people who attacked Daniel were the ones who knew him the best. That raises two points.

1. *It matters how you live.* People are watching you—yes, you. This means that it matters how you live. People who are watching you may one day be the ones attacking you. They watch how you live and see what kinds of decisions you make. They hear your conversations, they know how you conduct your business, and they know how you handle yourself in tough situations. It matters how you live every day.

Whether you're making multi-thousand-dollar decisions for your business or deciding what to serve at your next dinner party, make your decisions with the realization that your life is on display. There are so many subtle issues that come into play when making decisions, and many of them can't be put onto a spreadsheet and analyzed. Perhaps you could make your product cheaper somewhere else, or perhaps you could win political brownie points if you planned your dinner party a particular way, but I don't believe we make our best decisions until we pay careful attention to who and whose we are.

Carry yourself in the character of God; see yourself as the light of God. Make your decisions based on who you are in Christ so that when your attackers rise up, they will have to invent something to use against you.

2. *Do not give your attackers any ammunition.* The truth is, sometimes the accusations made against us are accurate. We give people the ammunition; we give them reason to come after us. It's not because we've done something right; it's because we've done something to legitimately tick them off.

Live your life in such a way that you don't give your attackers any ammo to use against you. As Ephesians 5:8 says, *"You were formerly darkness, but now you are Light in the Lord; walk as children of Light."* A bold stance in Christ usually draws enough attention by itself. Why would you want to do other things that could open you up to attack from others? You are light in the Lord. Walk like it.

I'm not proud to tell you this (but I guess I'll tell you anyway): It seems like I've made more mistakes in this area than I have done things right. I worked for a group of guys one time who were my friends, and later they became my attackers. They tried to micromanage me. They told me not to shout, "Woo-hooo! Woo!" when the band played a great song right before I spoke. Hey, that's the way music makes me feel. They said, "Don't do that. It makes the Bible study seem like a pep rally."

The crowd had been conditioned to yell "woo-hooo" with me every time I got up to speak. The night after my friends told me to cut it out, I got up and the whole crowd went crazy making all the noises while my attackers sat on the front row staring at me. Being the "Mister Passive-Aggressive" that I am, I sarcastically put my hand over my mouth and looked at them. The place went crazy again, and I just said, "My thoughts exactly."

That is a negative illustration. It's kind of funny, but it's the wrong way to handle a challenge. The way I handled it is the equivalent of poking a bear with a pencil. That was all the reason they needed to come after me. When I finished speaking, they were waiting for me locked and loaded. My point is, be careful how you choose to behave at work. Sooner or later, what you do will be used against you.

Comes before Success

> *Then this Daniel began distinguishing himself among the commissioners and satraps because he possessed an extraordinary spirit, and the king planned to appoint him over the entire kingdom.* (Daniel 6:3)

Daniel conducted himself in such a way that people noticed his character. This was a man who had compelling character. He carried the light well, and people were drawn to his light. The king even wanted to promote Daniel to a position over the entire kingdom. That's like being moved from the mailroom of a Fortune 500 company to a new corner office on the top floor! But read what happens at that moment: "*Then the commissioners and satraps began trying to find a ground of accusation against Daniel*" (Daniel 6:4).

Daniel's friends and coworkers came after him. When the attack begins, it's usually a sign that some kind of promotion is headed your way. Some of us spend our lives teetering on the brink of a compromise in our morality, our habits, or even in our relationships. The voice of compromise tries to tell us, "What difference does it make what I do in my dating life, how I spend my money, or how I do my business? Those who know me don't care!" The times we are most tempted to compromise are usually when we are on the front end of a God promotion.

When we choose to apply the life of God to the situations of our lives, we become a target of darkness. As long as we do not live out the life of

God, darkness considers us a harmless, not a hostile, enemy. But when we begin to live out the life of God, we become a threat to darkness.

God advances those who live out His life. But before the opportunity for promotion comes, we face an equal opportunity for compromise. In fact, we must be alert to the truth that when the opportunity for compromise comes, God's promotion is often just around the corner. Such opportunities for compromise generally show up as things we can willfully choose to do that are in violation of the will of God. Make no mistake, these opportunities are planned and presented by the enemy with the intended purpose of tripping us up and giving others ammunition to use against us.

In today's business world, there are many opportunities to compromise. Frequent and extended business travel opens the believer to potential compromise that no one would ever discover. Coed dormitories are the university norm; so it seems is the practice of sleepovers. Then there's the Internet, which has done more to make pornography easily accessible than any other form of distribution. Internet pornography continues to be the most profitable business on the Web. It's so profitable because it allows people to log on from the privacy of their own rooms and see whatever they desire—and no one has to know.

We may think that no one knows what we do on a business trip or in our college dorm room or while we are logged on to the Internet. True, they may not know the details, but they will see the lack of light. They will notice the lack of light because we have compromised the light by choosing darkness.

The ones who will see the loss of light the most will be those of us who compromise. If we could see even a glimpse of the promotion God has in store for us, no price would be too great to pay to protect it. The allure of compromise is lost when we get a consuming conviction that God has nothing but the best in store for us. If you are facing a moment of compromise, you must remember that success and promotion are close at hand and they are wrapped inside the life of God.

Chapter Twelve

Calls for a Subtle Shift

> *Then the commissioners and satraps began trying to find a ground of accusation against Daniel...but they could find no ground of accusation or evidence of corruption, inasmuch as he was faithful, and no negligence or corruption was to be found in him. Then these men said, "We will not find any ground of accusation against this Daniel unless we find it against him with regard to the law of his God."* (Daniel 6:4–5)

The attack is not always barefaced. It may not be as obvious as someone trying to get you fired from your job. It may actually come in a very subtle way. This was how Daniel's attackers came after him. There was nothing to accuse him of, because he was a man of character. They couldn't attack Daniel politically, because he had a faultless record. They couldn't attack his position, because he had served the king well and the king had promoted him largely based on the merit of his performance.

They couldn't find any ammunition to use against Daniel—so they attacked his spirituality. Their entire strategy was to use against him the one thing that they were certain he would do. They went before the king and said, "*All the commissioners of the kingdom, the prefects and the satraps, the high officials and the governors have consulted together that the king should establish a statute and enforce an injunction that anyone who makes a petition to any god or man besides you, O king, for thirty days, shall be cast into the lions' den*" (Daniel 6:7).

The king was tricked into cooperating with their plan to set up Daniel. They knew that Daniel would go to his home, open his windows, and pray to God. So a law was passed that didn't stop Daniel from praying but prohibited him from praying to his God. Do you see the subtlety? They didn't want to prohibit praying altogether. They weren't asking Daniel to renounce or deny God. They just set him up to fail because they knew he would go to his room, open his windows, and pray to God.

Daniel knew that people watched him through his windows during his prayer times. He could have gone to his room and prayed with his windows closed, and no one would have seen him. But for Daniel that would have been acknowledging that the king was someone equivalent with God and worthy to be prayed to. The subtle shift for Daniel would have been to continue his prayer time but to do it behind the privacy of closed windows. Instead he chose to continue to acknowledge his utter dependence on God rather than the laws of man.

The subtle shifts for all of us are the hardest to see and the easiest to slip into. We each have our issues that we can respond to publicly in faith or privately behind closed windows. It is the private display that all too often leads to a choice of convenience over character.

It Pushes You from Character to Convenience

What the attackers were trying to get Daniel to do was to move the basis of his decision from character to convenience. Here's the point: Sometimes it is going to cost you to be a man or woman of character. Living out of convenience doesn't cost anything. For Daniel, convenience would have said, "I don't want to offend anybody. I respect the king, so I'll pray privately. That way I don't mess up my promotion, and I still get to keep my commitment to pray."

Anytime your character comes under attack, it is with this kind of shift in mind. The idea is to get you out of living the life of God, the life of character, and into living a life of preference or convenience. Let me show you the difference.

Character	Convenience
Based on principle: "I'm going to obey the principles of God."	*Based on emotion:* "I'm going to do what I feel is best."
Based on God's will: "I'm going to do whatever God wants me to do."	*Based on pleasure:* "I'm going to do whatever brings me immediate pleasure."

Character	Convenience
Based on the future: "How will this impact my relationship with God and the rest of my life?"	*Based on the present:* "What should I do right now? I'm going to do whatever seems best to me at this moment."
Based on God's opinion: "What does God's Word say? What is the will of God for this situation?"	*Based on other people's opinions:* "What do other people say I should do? What is the popular thing to do?"
Based on sacrifice: "Even if it costs me position or opportunity, I'm going to do the right thing."	*Based on preference:* "This is what I prefer. This is how I prefer to handle it."

Your attackers will try to get you to move out of character and into convenience. We have all fallen for this at one time or another. Remember when you were young and you said, "I'll never do ___"? (You fill in the blank.) Then as you grew up, your friends changed and you started to do the things you said you would never do. It became convenient.

For many of us, the moment our friends change, our standards change, and we begin to do what is immediate and gives us the most pleasure. We find ourselves moving out of character and into convenience. These shifts happen when we move from college to the work world, from single to married, from one position to the next or one career to the next. They're subtle shifts. The reason they're subtle is because nobody will ever call us on them. No one will ever know. No one would have cared if Daniel had just shut his doors and prayed in private. But living a life of character costs.

Must Be Countered Strategically

Now when Daniel knew that the document was signed, he entered his house (now in his roof chamber he had windows

> *open toward Jerusalem); and he continued kneeling on his knees three times a day, praying and giving thanks before his God, as he had been doing previously.* (Daniel 6:10)

Daniel knew that the king had signed the law. He knew it could not be broken without penalty or overruled by any court in the land. But instead of compromising, Daniel continued praying just as he had been doing!

The best way to meet your attackers is to remain rooted in the character of God. Years ago a friend of mine in Houston was accused of doing something in his company that he was completely innocent of. He called me and said, "These people have accused me of something I didn't do. I'm under attack, and I'm innocent. Should I quit? You don't know what it's like, Dave. I walk down the hallway, and people won't speak to me; they won't even look me in the eye. When I walk into the break room, the conversation stops. I don't know how much I can take. Do you think I should leave?"

I hurt for my friend, but I told him he should stay and stand. If you're innocent, you've got to continue on in righteousness like Daniel did. It's not your job to even up the score.

Daniel did the right thing. He didn't try to take on every fight—just the one that really mattered. If you have to take on a fight, do it in a way that doesn't violate the presence of God inside you. You may feel like resorting to brute force, or you may be tempted to run away from the situation. But the best way to fight is to fight in a way that honors the life of God that is inside you.

Daniel continued to pray three times a day. He didn't turn his prayer time into a production but simply continued on as he always had, kneeling and praying toward Jerusalem. His friends watched and took note.

A crooked smile spread across their lips as they reminded the king of the new law. They took deep, personal satisfaction in casually dropping the information that Daniel had been breaking that law. Even the king couldn't override a law once it had been signed. Reluctantly, he gave the orders for Daniel to be thrown into the lions' den.

Daniel was taken to the den, and a large stone was rolled across the entrance. Daniel spent the night with the lions. The king spent the night pacing and hoping for Daniel's safety. Early the next morning, the king anxiously approached the lions' den and called out for Daniel: "Are you alive?" Read Daniel's response: "*My God sent His angel and shut the lions' mouths and they have not harmed me, inasmuch as I was found innocent before Him; and also toward you, O king, I have committed no crime*" (Daniel 6:22).

Imagine that verse being addressed to your attackers. The Lord God who stands on the side of those who live His character deals with all attackers. Daniel knew that regardless of what his attackers threw his way, God would preserve him and His own character. God doesn't build His character in us to destroy it but to release it so that those in darkness can observe it. God is in the business of creating life, giving life, and saving life through us.

> *The king then gave orders, and they brought those men who had maliciously accused Daniel, and they cast them, their children and their wives into the lions' den; and they had not reached the bottom of the den before the lions overpowered them and crushed all their bones*. (Daniel 6:24)

This is a gruesome Old Testament passage that shows that God defends the righteous. He may not throw your attackers into a lions' den, but Psalm 37:6 says, "*He will bring forth your righteousness as the light and your judgment as the noonday*." That means your choice to remain faithful and committed will one day be seen as clearly as the sun is seen in the high-noon sky and that your attackers will be taken care of. So don't quit!

Do you have someone in your life who you consider a donut person? Maybe you work for that kind of boss, and nothing is ever good enough. No matter what you do, he always has something negative to say. Maybe you grew up with what I call a "downer dad." You think your dad was put in your life to make you feel like the cause of all his problems. No matter what you do, it's never good enough.

Donut people tend to be people we clash with. They tend to be people who instantly bring out the very worst in us. Sometimes we can avoid them. Maybe we can transfer to work on another floor; perhaps we can drive another way to work or walk down another hall. Sometimes we just can't avoid them. Sometimes we have to face them and maintain character. That's why I've included the following strategy in this chapter.

The Procedure in the Attack

These principles come out of a book in the New Testament called Acts. Acts 4 tells the story of Peter and John, two disciples of Jesus. They were going around the country, preaching to the crowds about Jesus. They preached that Jesus, who died and now lives again, is the Son of God and the Messiah. They preached this message in a very dark and hostile environment.

> *As they were speaking to the people, the priests and the captain of the temple guard and the Sadducees came up to them, being greatly disturbed because they were teaching the people and proclaiming in Jesus the resurrection from the dead. And they laid hands on them and put them in jail until the next day, for it was already evening. But many of those who had heard the message believed; and the number of the men came to be about five thousand. On the next day, their rulers and elders and scribes were gathered together in Jerusalem; and Annas the high priest was there, and Caiaphas and John and Alexander, and all who were of high-priestly descent. When they had placed them in the center, they began to inquire, "By what power, or in what name, have you done this?"* (Acts 4:1–7)

Peter and John were going from town to town, preaching their simple message. This is still our core message today. It is the message of God for salvation, and He gives it tremendous power. The Sadducees were the bad guys. They were overly religious and extremely uptight. They had the temple guards seize Peter and John and throw them in prison for the night. The next morning, the Sadducees brought the disciples into an inquiry room filled with religious leaders. Peter and John stood right in the center of the room. Questions flew from everywhere as the religious leaders questioned the disciples' authority to speak the things they were saying. Fear, intimidation, potential punishment—all of these were a part of the experience. But Peter and John handled themselves and their accusers with grace. Let's see how they did it.

Anticipate Repercussions

> *As they were speaking to the people, the priests and the captain of the temple guard and the Sadducees came up to them, being greatly disturbed.... And they laid hands on them and put them in jail until the next day.* (Acts 4:1–3)

Peter and John came into the city and preached what they had been preaching everywhere else. But the religious leaders of this town saw the people listening and believing, and they decided some action needed to be taken in order to preserve their own influence. Anytime you do the right thing, get ready; you are going to experience something negative. *Every act of obedience will be attacked.* Get ready for the repercussions. Doing the right thing always brings out the donut people.

Answer with Results

> *But many of those who had heard the message believed; and the number of the men came to be about five thousand.* (Acts 4:4)

About five thousand people heard the disciples' message and believed, and one man was healed. The results spoke for themselves! The religious leaders of the town had maintained control over the people long enough. The time for freedom had come. The message was out; the people heard it; lives were changed, and so was the power base of the community. The next day Peter and John were taken before the highest religious rulers and questioned—but the results spoke for themselves.

The questions the religious leaders asked were meant to entrap the disciples. Instead of fighting back, instead of turning it into some chair-throwing, abuse-hurling, Jerry Springer guest spot, Peter and John let the results speak for themselves. "*And seeing the man who had been healed standing with them, they had nothing to say in reply*" (Acts 4:14). The donut people (uh, excuse me, the religious leaders) looked at the results and couldn't find anything to say.

We must always answer our critics with results. Don't take them on or try to fight them. That is not the Jesus principle. The Jesus way of handling an attack is to let your critics shoot words at you, let them take their shots at you, let them be as mean as they want to be; just answer them with results. In other words, let the results speak for themselves. If people do not like the way you do your work, let the fact that you are being successful in your work speak for itself. No one can deny success.

I teach a Bible study in Memphis on Monday nights. It has had many critics in the last year and a half. I have chosen not to take on the critics myself. That would only waste time and reinforce their position in their own minds. Instead, I have joined with the other Bible study leaders, and we have recommitted ourselves to doing what God has called us to do. We are committed to doing whatever it takes to create a place where people can connect with the presence of God. We will let the results speak for themselves. No one can deny twelve hundred people worshiping together.

Be Anchored in Righteousness

> *Then Peter, filled with the Holy Spirit, said to them, "Rulers and elders of the people...there is salvation in no one else; for there is no other name under heaven that has been given among men by which we must be saved."* (Acts 4:8, 12)

Righteousness is a long, eleven-dollar Bible word, but it simply means "to be in right standing." The donut people didn't know what to do with Peter and John. They tried to bait the disciples into overreacting or defending themselves in a way that could be used against them. If they messed up, Peter and John could have been thrown back in jail. Instead, these two guys stayed anchored in righteousness and handled the attack the right way. Peter spoke calmly, confidently, and cautiously—and it paid off.

The leaders observed Peter's confidence and saw that he stayed anchored in righteousness; he didn't let his emotions speak. They began to recognize that these men had been with Jesus. Peter and John took on their critics properly, and the result was that the donut people saw Jesus. This is the point. It's not important that you and I get vindication or prove our point or win the argument. It *is* important that the donut people in our lives see the Lord Jesus in the way we handle their criticism and attacks.

Does anchoring your response in righteousness mean that you can never get angry? No. It means that when you do get angry, it had better be a righteous anger. It had better not be some sort of psychotic, emotional anger. In other words, ask yourself, "Would God be angry about what I'm angry about? Is this something that Jesus would be angry about?" I know that advice sounds like it ought to be on a Bible school finger-paint poster, but too many of us have a short fuse. If someone criticizes us, we explode. On a scale from one to ten with ten representing the explosion point, many of us live at about a nine or nine-and-a-half. So you have to ask yourself, "Can I be angry about this and still be in a relationship with God? Or am I going to have to put God on hold and push Him aside so that I can go be a jerk to the jerks?"

Abandon Retreat

> *And when they had summoned them, they commanded them not to speak or teach at all in the name of Jesus. But Peter and John answered and said to them, "Whether it is right in the sight of God to give heed to you rather than to God, you be the judge; for we cannot stop speaking about what we have seen and heard."* (Acts 4:18–20)

The religious leaders still had Peter and John in front of them. They tried to intimidate them; it didn't work. They tried to scare them; that didn't work either. The results were obvious, and the popularity of these two men was growing. So their attackers decided to acknowledge it all. They said, "You guys have had a great time! Five thousand people responded to your invitation, and one man was healed. Not a bad meeting! Where are you headed next? I mean, we think the people here have heard enough, so you shouldn't speak here anymore. In fact, you're through here."

How did Peter and John respond? They simply said, "We are not going to abandon the truth. We are not going to retreat. Being quiet is not an option. Compromising our message is not an option. Whether that is right or wrong in your eyes, you will have to be the judge. But as for us, we can't stop doing what God has started to do in us, and we can't stop speaking about it."

There was no option of retreat. It wasn't even a consideration. They took the stance of no compromise. This is how we are to live.

People never criticize my theology or my outlines. They only criticize my jokes, which actually don't mean anything; they're just jokes. I was speaking in Texas, and a guy came up to me and wanted to "exhort me in the Lord." That's Christian-eze for "I am about to take my messed up life and project it on you." He "exhorted" me about some of the jokes I told on the subject of telemarketers.

I had done a rant about people who call my house wanting to sell me stuff. Sometimes when they call, I make them read their little prepared speech all the way through twice, and then I say, "Can you say that again? I wasn't listening."

People call from Sprint wanting me to switch long-distance carriers, and I say, "You're with Sprint; I'm with MCI—how about we both switch? I'll sign on your deal if you sign on my deal!" *Click.*

These were just silly jokes. My jokes aren't leveled at anybody; they just build a premise to help people get into the Bible study. Well, this guy told me how offended he was that I made jokes at the expense of telemarketers. I asked him, "Are you a telemarketer?" He replied, "Well, no." So I asked, "Then what's the problem?" He said, "Uh, I was just offended. I have friends who are telemarketers."

He was talking in circles. Then he started to tell me why telling jokes like those wasn't biblical. He began to quote verses. I found myself being riddled with scripture bullets from all over the Bible.

My tendency has always been to fold, shrink away, and say, "Oh, please, I didn't mean to hurt anybody." But this time, while the scripture shrapnel was flying past me, something clicked. I sensed that I could take this guy on without compromising my relationship with God and without being emotional or in the flesh. So I said to him, "I appreciate your insight. I never thought about the jokes like that. At the same time, let me say one thing before you go. I hope you don't treat your pastor the way you just treated me."

He didn't quite know how to respond, so I calmly helped him see the point. "Every pastor and every guy you hear speak carries a certain anointing," I said. "They hold a certain office within the kingdom, and even though you don't approve of everything they say, you don't have the right to be mean and pick on people in the service of the kingdom of God. Even if you don't approve of the jokes and you don't care for the style, you don't have the right to pick on people and tear them down. I hope you don't pull your pastor aside and 'exhort' him in the way you 'exhorted' me, because you don't have any idea what it is like to carry this kind of call or what it takes to do this sort of thing." Now the guy really didn't know what to say. My spirit said quietly to itself, "Great job!"

When the donut people attack, you don't have to run away or collapse under their intimidation, and you don't have to be critical in return. Rather, in the confidence of the Lord, you can hold your ground.

Accept Rewards

Taking on the donut people in a godly way produces some really amazing rewards. First of all, people get to see the light of God operating in you. Some people have been turned off from God and the church because all they have ever seen are Christian donut people. Many people have grown up not being able to catch a glimpse of God because the very people who claim to know God block anyone from seeing Him in their lives.

The second reward is that you get to carry out the will of God. These men in Acts 4 carried out the will of God in the right way. They didn't do it by being hateful or mean. They did it in a way that caused their accusers to see their confidence in God's ability and back down. Carrying out the will of God brings you into the greatest and safest adventures you can imagine. When you are carrying out God's will, you have the security of knowing that the plan will not fail. And you know there will always be enough resources to accomplish anything God sets out for you to do.

If you happen to be in an interim period when there are no donut people in your life, enjoy it. One day soon there will be a pastry critic who will pass through and level an attack at you. I hope you keep these lessons on how to live with donut people close to your heart. You will need them.

On the way to work or school or running errands, stop at your favorite pastry shop and order your favorite item. Hold it in both hands and take a big bite out of it. As you smile and chew, tell yourself that the donut people in your life will not get the best of you.

THIRTEEN

Stay *Lit*

GETTING OUT OF DOUBT

There is a sign that hangs over our heads. This sign is lighted only at certain times. When it's illuminated, it says "goober." The sign lights up when we feel awkward, embarrassed, and self-conscious.

When I was in junior high, this sign flashed on and off so frequently that it looked like a strobe light. One time in high school, I bought a milk shake, put it on top of my car while I got in, and left it there as I pulled out of the parking lot. Everybody in the restaurant was pointing. I waved back, "Yeah, I know I have a cool car. Thanks!" and drove on. As I pulled up to a stop at an intersection, the shake spilled all over the windshield. That sign popped up over my head and flashed on and off. Everybody at the light pointed and laughed. Thinking quickly, I rolled down my window and yelled, "Hey, did anybody else see the size of that bird?"

Not long ago I spoke at a university Bible study. About three hundred students filled a tiny, old gymnasium. The band led worship, and as each song flowed into the next, the worship became more intense and intimate. I was standing in the back of the room. The band played the last song, then I was up to speak. As I moved from the back toward the stage, my foot caught on the power cord for the lights. I yanked the plug out of the wall. The room went totally black—which made it easier for everyone to see my sign.

We all have goober moments. Maybe you've been out to dinner with some friends. The four of you were sitting in a booth, enjoying yourselves. You moved in the vinyl seat, and it made that sound—you know, the one that makes everyone look at you and snicker. You spent the rest of the evening trying to re-create that sound just to prove it didn't come out of you.

When the goober moments come, laugh. I promise you'll live through them.

Just as you are certain to have goober moments, there will be times when you will have doubt. All of us go through certain situations that cause us to doubt: the businessperson with the death of a dream; the teenager with the loss of a friend; the husband with the loss of a job; the couple facing a broken marriage. The adult experiencing a mid-life crisis who asks, "What am I doing?" The mom with the prodigal child who wonders, "Is this Christian-life thing really true?" The disillusioned believer who cries, "Have I just been good for no apparent reason?" The failed magician who ponders, "Has this all just been a hoax?"

There have been times in my own life when I've wondered if there really is a God. When the unthinkable appears in our lives—and it will—trust turns to doubt, and our sense of direction, protection, and confidence is shaken.

Doubt is not the lack of trust. The essence of doubt is being caught between two different beliefs at the same time. I've spoken at a lot of ski retreats, and the slopes always look absolutely beautiful from my hotel window. My room always seems to be just above the beginner slope, so I get to watch everyone learn how to ski. Almost to a person, the beginning skiers start down the slope with their skis taking on a life of their own. Each ski heads off in a different direction until the people are split so far that they fall backward with their skis in the air. That's the way doubt makes us feel. We feel caught between two beliefs and unable to do anything to stop the progress, so we just fall down.

This was exactly what was happening to John the Baptist. His heart was divided. He knew that his ministry was to precede the ministry of the Messiah. But it appeared that his life would soon be taken. Did he run his course? Was his life what it should have been? Or did he miss the mark?

> *When Jesus had finished giving instructions to His twelve disciples, He departed from there to teach and preach in their cities. Now when John, while imprisoned, heard of the works of Christ, he sent word by his disciples and said to Him, "Are You the Expected One, or shall we look for someone else?"* (Matthew 11:1–3)

John was asking, "Jesus, have I lived my whole life for a myth? Have I laid my life on the line for something that is not true? Are you really the One? Or should we look for someone else?" Darkness had positioned itself close enough to John to de-create all that God had done in and through his ministry. What the enemy wanted most was to choke the faith out of John. John was locked in his struggle to stay *lit*.

Good theology is what pulls you through a time of doubt. John had to reach deep into all that he had believed and preached in order to silence the rising panic. What he had proven to be true through the living of his life, he now held on to with all his mental might. Even this was challenged by his circumstances.

Knowing theology is not enough. In order for us to find the strength to face our challenges, we must own theology at the deepest levels of our lives. It's like eating a meal prepared by a gourmet chef; the food must be tasted, eaten, and digested before it becomes part of the body. Our emotions must submit to theology. If they don't, they will run out of control and lead us into uncertainty, guilt, and fantasy.

Jesus' response to John was strategic. He didn't say, "John, stay right there. I'm going to come and put my arm around you. It's going to be OK." He didn't have the Florida Boys come to his cell, break into a big southern gospel concert, and sing "I'll Fly Away." He didn't send a little greeting card with a Scripture verse on the bottom of it. Do you know what Jesus did? He told John's disciples, "You send him My word."

Jesus answered and said to them, "Go and report to John what you hear and see: the blind receive sight and the lame walk, the lepers are cleansed and the deaf hear, the dead are raised up, and the poor have the gospel preached to them. And blessed is he who does not take offense at Me." (Matthew 11:4–6)

Reading this might not make much sense at first because the message Jesus sent to John was in Old Testament code. When John heard these words, he knew exactly what they meant. Let me give you a modern paraphrase of this verse. Imagine that you are John, facing a moment of intense doubt, and Jesus sends you a letter that reads:

John,

I am the Christ,
in control and committed.
Love,

Jesus

Imagine that John was sitting in his cell and this card was slid under his cell door. When he read what Jesus had written to him, this is what he heard: (1) Jesus is the Christ, (2) Jesus is in control, and (3) Jesus is committed to him and his situation, no matter how bad it looks. These three things are as important to us today as they were to John the Baptist because they reassure us of Christ's character. Our assurance in the midst of doubt depends on our grasp of the character of Jesus.

Jesus made Himself the issue. When doubt comes, the issue is never the circumstances we face; it is our grasp of His character in our lives. In times of doubt, we are faced with two options: to forfeit everything we have lived for or to go back to the foundation of our faith—the character of God Himself.

Os Guinness, in his book *God in the Dark*, calls this the "Square One Principle." He explains, "If we give up then we abandon faith altogether. But if we go back to Square One we will find a faith that is solid and secure. The lesson of the Square One Principle is this: the person who has the courage to go back when necessary is the one who goes on in the end."[1] We must go back to the basics before going forward.

He Is the Christ

> *The blind receive sight and the lame walk, the lepers are cleansed and the deaf hear, the dead are raised up, and the poor have the gospel preached to them.* (Matthew 11:5)

Jesus reminded John of who He was. I know it feels different from this, but doubt is primarily about who our trust is in. John sat alone in that dungeon with all the props of his life knocked out from under him. Even though the letter was quite brief, Jesus identified Himself as the Messiah.

Jesus was quoting from Isaiah 61:1: "*The Spirit of the Lord GOD is upon me, because the LORD has anointed me to bring good news to the afflicted; He has sent me to bind up the brokenhearted, to proclaim liberty to captives and freedom to prisoners.*" This Old Testament passage is a messianic verse. John knew that whoever was able to perform these acts was indeed the Messiah. As John read these words from his cell, I'm sure the message he heard was, "My dear brother, I am the Christ. You have put your faith in the right guy."

Jesus is legit. He is the real deal. He is the Messiah. He fulfilled every one of the Old Testament prophecies about the Messiah. We need to let the legitimacy of Jesus penetrate our lives. When it does, it puts a "no-stick" surface on our souls. Doubt has a much harder time finding a place to stick. When this truth penetrates our lives, we find the beginnings of a trust that will allow us to live authentically in the midst of doubt. A trust that stands in the face of doubt is a faith grounded in the truth of who Christ is.

He Is in Control

> *Go and report to John what you hear and see.* (Matthew 11:4)

Jesus reminded John that He is in control of circumstances. Regardless of how things appear, He is still the ruler. In verse 4, Jesus was speaking of His present demonstration of power. John's disciples had followed Jesus for several days just to observe His ministry. They had seen many miracles and had heard Him speak. They had seen Him rule and reign over all kinds of sickness and pain. Christ's ministry was powerfully at work.

The focus of Jesus' ministry was to make the kingdom of God visible. He overcame the darkness by healing the wounded. When John's eyes fell upon these words, he heard Jesus say, "John, the kingdom is advancing. All is going as planned. You have done your part; you introduced Me well."

He Is Committed

> *And blessed is he who does not take offense at Me.* (Matthew 11:6)

To put this verse another way, "Don't be offended by the Lord." It would have been easy for John to stumble over Jesus. Doubt is hard and lonely, and John felt it intensely. He was still a young man, not old and useless. Yet he had lived as he was told to live, spoke what he was told to speak. And the apparent reward was to be thrown in jail and ultimately relieved of his head. All the while Jesus walked freely about the land.

Doubt and unbelief are not the same things. At this point, John was not in a state of unbelief; he was not willfully refusing to believe. Rather, his expectations were colliding with his doubt. If his doubt had not been properly confronted, it could have grown into unbelief. The same is true for any of us. When some of our expectations about God are not met, it's easy to take offense and say, "Why didn't God do…?" Or, "Why did God allow that to happen?" Or, "If this is the way God treats his people…"

It would be easy to believe that God is mad, angry, unfair, disgusted, uninterested, and indifferent toward us. In reality, God is understanding, aware, present, involved, working, and committed. Theology and feelings are connected. In a season of doubt, we must let what we know invade what we feel.

When John read this line of the letter, he could hear Jesus saying, "John, even though the dungeon of doubt is dark and you will suffer, know that I am committed to you."

Believe it or not, I can hear your thoughts. You are saying, "Right! That sounds good. That sounds very sweet and devotional, but is it real? And does it work?" I want to tell you how knowing these three things about Jesus brought me through a major time of doubt.

I met a girl, and I totally fell for her. Her name was Nezi. She was a "G3"—godly, gorgeous, and great. A believer who had led each one of her family members to Christ, she was a sharp, very articulate lawyer with her own law practice in downtown Rio de Janeiro. (I had to go to South America to get a date, but that's a whole other story.) She was my interpreter for an eight-day revival sponsored by First Baptist Church in Rio. I spoke in all the schools in the area, and I taught Bible studies in the towns from house to house. And everywhere I went, Nezi went—which was kind of like having a first date that went on for over a week. Very cool!

I returned to Brazil about six months later, and she was my interpreter once again. The more time I spent with her, the more respect I had for her, and the more I was drawn to her. We spoke at a school, where I told the students who Jesus is and what He has done. I talked about how awesome He is and explained that if you give your life to Him, your life will be different forever. I gave an invitation, and 110 students stood up. I thought, *That couldn't be right. They must have thought I said, "Who wants free pizza?"*

So I had them all sit down, and I started all over again. When I got to the point where I would give the invitation, I said to Nezi, "You don't need me; you just give it." She stood up, and I sat down. She started giving the invitation in Portuguese, and 110 students stood up again. It was amazing!

A woman who knows the things of God and how to communicate them. Wow! That is very attractive to me. Besides that, she could speak English, but not enough to argue. Perfect! No stress, no fighting. Low maintenance.

Chapter Thirteen

On my third trip to Brazil, I made sure I had about four days off—just to be with Nezi. She drove me all around Rio and took me to eat at a little restaurant that jutted out into the Atlantic Ocean. If you've ever been to Rio or seen pictures of the city, you know that in the middle of the city is a big Christ statue. It's 120 feet tall, sitting on a mountain that's two thousand feet high. Christ has His arms out, and they are forty-eight feet across. We walked up the 220 steps to the base of the statue. The mid-afternoon sun cast a shadow of Christ across us. That was the first place I ever kissed her. There couldn't be a better Christian date. To kiss her in the shadow of Jesus and His outstretched arms! That was the coolest date of my life.

I left there telling her, "I'm going to bring you to America in December. I do a lot of conferences, and I want you to see the ministry and what I do in America." I kept in touch by phone—at a dollar a minute—anticipating our time together.

One day I had just finished packing for a series of conferences and had my bags in my hands to head to the airport when I got a call from one of my missionary friends in Brazil. He said, "Dave, I'm calling about Nezi." I said, "Yeah, she's great, isn't she?" He said, "No, you don't understand. Yesterday in downtown traffic, someone reached into her car window and cut her throat."

I never saw her again.

I had to drive to the airport, stand up in those youth conferences, and talk about how great Jesus is. I won't lie to you; it was the darkest time of my life. I told God, "I work for You. You are all-powerful and all-knowing. You know what the deal is. You could have protected her or stopped that from happening."

It was the three things I knew about Jesus that pulled me through that time of doubt. I was long past needing some emotional experience or some new song. I didn't need someone hugging me and telling me, "It's going to be OK." I had to get up every day that month and speak twenty-seven times, knowing that she was supposed to be with me. I had to boldly proclaim the gospel while I was fighting doubt in my own personal life.

It was very difficult for me not to just walk away from everything. The only way I got through the crisis was to sit down and begin and end my day moving through those three things. I put my trust in the right Person. He is who He says He is. I haven't lived my life for a myth. Just because someone I loved dearly was murdered does not make it all a myth.

I know Jesus is real because He is the Christ. He is in control, and He is committed. He is who He says He is. I believe it. I've allowed that truth to sink deep into my life. I understand that it may cost me and test me to my last thread. I may not be able to take it, but it is still true.

At those times when we feel powerless, we must remember that God hears the powerless. Their prayers are answered. At the deepest moments of doubt, at our weakest moments, that is where the presence of God is. The powerless are always heard, and the questioners are always answered.

Jesus came for those who are in situations where doubt and questions are combined with fear and panic. We must live our lives in such a way that people can see His character in us and through us. The world in darkness longs to see if this Christ really is who He says He is. They long to see a life that proves He is who we say He is. They ache to watch character in action.

I don't know your pain. I only know mine. But hopefully through the sharing of my victory over doubt, you can find the confidence to believe that Christ is who He says He is. Hopefully you can find the strength to persevere.

Perseverance is possible. Because of these events in my life, I am able to stand in front of students and tell them the truth. Perseverance is possible. You can go on.

There are still times when the weather is right or I hear a certain song that I think of Nezi. It might be a place that reminds me of where I used to sit and talk with her. All the emotions are set off again. But what pulls me through those dark times is the light of Christ. John the Baptist must have seen it in the dark cell, just before he was beheaded.

I have seen that light in my darkest times. If you look—just look—you'll see it too.

Throughout the centuries many have attempted to extinguish the light. But there has always been a witness to the character and life of Christ. The darkness has never and never will be able to overcome the light of the life found in Jesus Christ. "*From the days of John the Baptist until now the kingdom of heaven suffers violence, and violent men take it by force*" (Matthew 11:12).

The battle John faced in the darkness of his prison cell while he awaited death is the same battle Jesus faced on the cross while dying. It is the same battle you and I face daily as we seek to flesh out the life of Christ in a world that seeks to overcome us. The kingdom of heaven has always suffered attacks, but it has always prevailed.

Victory for God's kingdom of light is assured when you and I take our place in the battle of light against darkness. To the extent that we embrace the character of Christ, we determine the success of the light in this world.

You are the light of the world! Get *lit*. Stay *lit*.

Love, Dave

Tell a friend about a time when you felt like a goober. Let it remind you that God is ever present and in control of every situation you face.

Study Guide

Chapter 1

For Group Discussion

1. Why is Sunday the only spiritual day of the week for many people?
2. Why are people so unwilling to think spiritually throughout the week?
3. What's the incentive for building character?
4. How do we understand the tension between the pain in the world and the fact that God has won the battle?
5. How did Jesus win the battle over evil?
6. What's the goal of the Christian life?

For Individual Reflection

1. What's the biggest battle that you are fighting spiritually?
2. What holds you back from developing spiritually?
3. Who's responsible for the evil in your life?
4. Why do you suffer if God loves you?
5. "I must be good so others will see Jesus in my life and trust in Him." Is this a right attitude? Why or why not?
6. Will you stay like you are, or will you choose to be *lit*?

Chapter 2

For Group Discussion

1. Discuss the role of sin as it relates to our world's need for the character of Christ.
2. Comment on this statement: "Character is choosing what is right; it's about following the rules."
3. Who does the work of making people better?
4. Do you think that anyone could do any sin, however wicked, or do you think that only certain people could do really horrible sins? For example, could *anyone* rape or kill or abuse innocent victims, or are only certain wicked people capable of such acts?
5. "People sin through ignorance." Is this right?
6. Given what we've learned in chapter 2, comment on the importance of Christian political involvement.

For Individual Reflection

1. When do you feel furthest from God?
2. When do you feel closest to God?
3. What sins do you struggle with the most?
4. What sorrow in your life has helped you to see your need for God more clearly?
5. Do you feel more free when you pray or when you sin?
6. In the process of reading this chapter, did you abandon any thoughts you used to hold as true?

Chapter 3

For Group Discussion

1. What's the purpose of history?
2. What work is God doing?
3. How should seeing each other as a family change our attitude about Christian relationships?
4. Share with each other your conversion stories.
5. Who initiates the process of salvation?
6. What must precede a commitment to Christ?

For Individual Reflection

1. Of the four roles listed in this chapter, which one do you most play in life?
2. How does understanding the process of redemption encourage you?
3. Where have you pulled away from Christ's life-changing power?
4. Do you feel the total freedom of Christ? In what way?
5. Could you identify with Anne Lamott's story of her conversion? How so?
6. Which person in your life most needs Jesus Christ? In what way?

Chapter 4

For Group Discussion

1. After God does the work of salvation in us, what work should we be doing?
2. How are you trapped by antiquated church language?
3. Why do people hide behind stock expressions and written formulae?
4. Is political activism a cop-out for not Christianizing the world?
5. Should we tell people who don't know Jesus that the things they're doing are wrong?
6. Do most Christians live in freedom, or do they feel trapped?

For Individual Reflection

1. What aspect of Christ's life—incarnation to glorification—struck you when reading this chapter?
2. What pet peeve must be abandoned because of what you've learned?
3. How will you dedicate yourself to living the light of Christ?
4. In what way do you abandon yourself to trivial issues because you're afraid to confront people with the gospel?
5. What spiritual issues are disrupting your development of Christ's character?
6. How is a Christian moral?

Chapter 5

For Group Discussion

1. Think of popular television and radio advertisements. What do they say about what our society values? (Think of specific examples.)

2. In what way does personal life affect prayer life?
3. In whom or what do we trust: God, or specific promises that He has given us in Scripture? What's the difference?
4. Why do we pray? What's the point of it?
5. Share with each other answered prayers that came only after a significant length of time. (For some of you, that may be only a couple of days!)
6. Can people trust in God without knowing Him personally?

For Individual Reflection

1. What's your bottom line?
2. What *specifically* is keeping you from having an effective prayer life?
3. Whom do you trust more than you trust Christ? Who competes with Christ for your affections?
4. In what area of your life is it hardest for you to trust Christ?
5. Why don't you pray as much as you say you want to pray?
6. What passage of the Bible most moves you to love and trust God? Read that passage as a prayer to Him now.

Chapter 6

For Group Discussion

1. Is a Christian permitted to smoke cigarettes or drink alcohol?
2. Why is living in Christian freedom so difficult in our Christian culture? Should it be that way?
3. Is sin rule *making* or rule *breaking*?
4. What's the danger of criticizing a new Christian's behavior?
5. Is Christ included in the believer's life, or is the believer included in Christ's life? (Support your argument with Scripture.)
6. What's the most important thing you can pray for another believer—for a better moral life or that he or she would love Christ more?

For Individual Reflection

1. What do you do only in private because you fear that other people will criticize you for it?
2. What's something that you don't do—and you're really proud that you don't do it?
3. Is your life characterized more by rules or by freedom?

4. What's the cause of your anxieties? Is it that you fear that you can't, won't, or aren't living up to someone's standards? What's the solution?
5. Are you willing to abandon your pursuit of being good and let Christ be your all in all?
6. Is God more pleased with you when you do well or when you turn to Him brokenhearted, like a child?

Chapter 7

For Group Discussion

1. Is it possible to want things that are pleasant in this world (status, money, a nice house) and still desire the things of Christ (service, prayer, reading the Bible)?
2. In what specific areas are Christians today most tempted to compromise?
3. Why are some people who don't know Christ just as moral as some Christians?
4. Can Christians actually follow their hearts? Should they know that they're doing wrong just by their feelings?
5. How does God judge a community? An individual?
6. How can Christians change a society?

For Individual Reflection

1. In what area of your life are you a practical atheist?
2. Are you hardhearted?
3. In what area of life do you most want to live your own way?
4. How is God using you to change the world?
5. What's the most important thing you can do as a Christian today?
6. Are you willing to be *lit*—again, or perhaps for the first time—by the flame of Christ?

Chapter 8

For Group Discussion

1. What is being *lit* all about?
2. Who is at the center of a person whose life is *lit?*
3. Who is the only person—ever—who has walked with integrity and worked righteousness? How do we appropriate that person's life?

4. Is character about what we do or about what's done to us?
5. How do we know if someone is a person of character?
6. Are Christians in America generous in the way that they should be?

For Individual Reflection

1. What do you want in a partner that you don't have in yourself?
2. Do you know that Christ is your friend, living in you?
3. Do you desire to know Christ more than you desire things that might captivate you for a moment but leave you empty?
4. Are you as determined to be godly as you are to be a good student or a good athlete?
5. In what way can you identify with the life of David?
6. Are you ready to start afresh?

Chapter 9

For Group Discussion

1. What strains a believer's relationship with God more than anything else?
2. Is a person's biggest problem a lack of spiritual guidance or just plain disobedience?
3. How does the vertical relationship influence the horizontal? Does the horizontal influence the vertical?
4. What must change before a person's actions change?
5. How do we know when God is working in our lives to change parts of our character?
6. What's the big work God is doing right now around the world?

For Individual Reflection

1. What life strategies have you had to abandon because they only brought you pain?
2. As you read this book, where is God working the most in your life?
3. Can you feel God at work in you?
4. What's the goal of obedience?

5. What specific, new desire has God given you that you could not have had before you became a Christian?
6. What new desire are you praying that Christ will give you so that you can better serve Him?

Chapter 10

For Group Discussion

1. Why be good?
2. When does the battle for holiness end?
3. How are Christians light for the world?
4. The person, passion, and power of God—which of these is the emphasis of your church right now?
5. Do most Christians live by different standards and priorities than the world?
6. Should Christians be living by any rules at all? Or only by the Holy Spirit in them?

For Individual Reflection

1. What do you need to give up to simplify your life?
2. Is your hectic routine simply part of a master plan to show God that you're worthy of His love?
3. In what way do you know that your Christian life is supernatural?
4. Who is first in your priorities? (Honestly.)
5. For you, what is success? At what point in your life would you be willing to say to yourself, "Now I have done well"?
6. How will you live or think differently after reading this chapter?

Chapter 11

For Group Discussion

1. How do we really know if God approves of something or not?
2. If given two options, both of which seem right, how do we know which one to take?
3. Is an action right before God if we do it only because we think it's right, even if we don't feel right about doing it?

4. Within the group, think of five hypothetical situations involving two choices that are not sinful. Discuss how a person would think through the issues when choosing between the two competing goods.
5. When David didn't kill Saul, was he following a rule, or was he submitting to God's timing and leadership?
6. How can David's example be followed today?

For Individual Reflection

1. When you want to know if something is right, do you more often turn to friends or to Scripture?
2. Reflect on a wrong decision that you made. Looking back, were there any warning signs that you should've seen?
3. Do you talk to God about the decisions that you're facing?
4. What's one decision that you've been slow to talk to God about?
5. When has someone hurt you because he or she was telling you what to do rather than giving you godly counsel? Or was that person giving you godly counsel and you just responded selfishly?
6. Be honest—are you more like David or are you more like Saul?

Chapter 12

For Group Discussion

1. Have you ever invited a non-Christian to a Christian event—only to regret that you'd brought him or her? Why?
2. Do people who say they love Christ but don't ever show Christ's love actually love Him?
3. Have you ever had someone attack you because you love and trust Christ? Share your story with the group.
4. Can we find happiness apart from doing what's right?
5. Is it OK for the Christian to work for rewards?
6. Have you ever failed to support a fellow believer when he was under attack for his beliefs? Share your story with the group.

For Individual Reflection

1. Do you work with jerks, or are you the jerk people work with?
2. Are you happy?

3. What offends people about your life? Is it the gospel?
4. Name one area of your life where you interact with people and find it hard not to hurt others.
5. Now name one area of your life where you can be hurt in interaction with others.
6. Are questions 4 and 5 related? In other words, how does how you hurt others relate to how you are hurt by others?

Chapter 13

For Group Discussion

1. What is the essence of doubt? Is it lack of trust?
2. When John asked if Jesus was the Messiah, Jesus answered that John should look at all that He was doing. How does the historical testimony about Christ influence our view of Him?
3. What was the focus of Jesus' ministry? Why did He come?
4. "I put my trust in the right person." Is knowing Christ enough to get us through the difficult times? If so, how? If not, why follow Him?
5. How can we encourage each other if each person's pain is his or her own?
6. How can anyone find meaning in this life?

For Individual Reflection

1. When do you doubt God the most?
2. Do you know that Christ came to live and to die for you?
3. What has been the darkest moment of your life? How did God bring you closer to Him through it?
4. Are you in a dark place or a good place right now?
5. When do you feel saddest? When do you feel happiest? How does Christ meet you during both of those times?
6. Can you go on? How? Why?

Notes

Chapter 1

1. A. T. Robertson, *Word Pictures in the New Testament* (Grand Rapids, Mich.: Baker Book House, 1930), 33.

2. Donald A. Hagner, *Word Biblical Commentary* (Nashville, Tenn.: Word Incorporated, 1993), 68.

Chapter 2

1. Dallas Willard, *The Spirit of the Disciplines: Understanding How God Changes Lives* (San Francisco: Harper, 1991), 45.

2. Philip Friedman, ed., *Martyrs and Fighters: The Epic of the Warsaw Ghetto* (New York: Praeger, 1954), 166–167.

Chapter 3

1. Anne Lamott, *Traveling Mercies: Some Thoughts on Faith* (New York: Random House, 1999), 48–50.

Chapter 4

1. Dietrich Bonhoeffer, *Letters and Papers from Prison* (New York: McMillan, 1971), 88.

Chapter 6

1. Mike Williams, "You Might Be Religious If…" (Lakeland, Fla: self-published) You can contact Mike at www.christiancomedian.com.

Chapter 11

1. Douglas V. Porpora, *Landscape of the Soul* (New York: Oxford Press, 2001), 8.

Chapter 13

1. Os Guinness, *God in the Dark: The Assurance of Faith Beyond a Shadow of Doubt* (Wheaton, Ill.: Crossway Books, 1996), 18.